"If you're a parent, chances are one of  child will be sexually assaulted—and give we see and hear plenty of sickening accou their new book, however, Drs. Robinson an ....courage you not to live in fear, but to equip yourself and your kids with the awareness and skills that will help keep them safe."

—Jim Daly, president, Focus on the Family

"This book is a weapon against the enemy of your child's heart and soul. It's a shield to protect them from known and unknown predators. It will enable you to parent not out of fear but confidently. It's such a practical and empowering book!"

—Chris Fabry, author and host of *Chris Fabry Live*

"This book should be a desk reference for every parent, pastor, church leader, school administrator, teacher, and anyone who works with children. The authors do a fantastic job of equipping parents to foster a 'warrior's heart' in their children."

—Camille Cates, author, speaker, ACBC certified counselor

"*Protecting Your Child from Predators* was an absolute eye-opener for me. Robinson and Scott made me aware of the dangers our children face. Full of practical tips for sleepovers, camps, and neighborhood bike rides. This book is a must-read for every parent to keep their children safe and strong."

—Sam Chan, City Bible Forum, Australia

"In our world today, this book is necessary and sobering. It was especially helpful in breaking down age groups, giving specific examples of how predators work. It is our moral and Christian responsibility to be informed, take action, and do our very best to protect all who are at risk. This resource is needed in every home, school, and church."

—Lisa Crump, vice-president volunteer mobilization and liaison to prayer ministries, National Day of Prayer Task Force

"At a time when we're becoming increasingly aware of the prevalence of sexual abuse, we need the guidance Drs. Robinson and Scott provide in this long-overdue resource. Parents will be thankful for the safeguards presented here to protect their children and teens from life-altering abuse. And so will the children in your care."

—Sally Gary, director, CenterPeace,
and author of *Loves God, Likes Girls*

"*Protecting Your Child from Predators* is one of the most comprehensive and helpful books on abuse written specifically for parents. It's the perfect balance of factual research, personal stories, and application for each stage of your child's development. This book will help prevent abuse."

—Jimmy Hinton, MDiv, minister and abuse advocate,
Somerset Church of Christ, JimmyHinton.org

"Sadly, whether it is a doctor, teacher, or most regrettably, a member of the clergy, child sexual abuse is plaguing our sexually saturated culture. Love your children and grandchildren by protecting them. This book is a great tool for you to prepare now or run the risk of counseling later."

—Corey Miller, PhD, president/CEO, Ratio Christi

"Our worst nightmare—someone we love, especially a child, experiences any form of sexual abuse. And we find out years later, which finally explains the acting out, the hiding, the sudden shift in personality, but doesn't do a thing for our sense of helplessness and horror that it occurred under our watch. Drs. Beth Robinson and Latayne Scott provide a no-nonsense guide to facing this difficult subject unflinchingly. Their suggestions are clear and concise. Their approach is sensitive yet direct. This is a must-have guide for anyone who has charge of raising a human being—a needed support for navigating these difficult waters of an all too pervasive plague—predators."

—Patti Rokus, author/artist of RocksTellStories.com

PROTECTING
YOUR
CHILD
FROM
PREDATORS

PROTECTING
YOUR
CHILD
FROM
PREDATORS

HOW TO RECOGNIZE AND RESPOND
TO SEXUAL DANGER

BETH ROBINSON, EdD, AND
LATAYNE C. SCOTT, PhD

BETHANYHOUSE
a division of Baker Publishing Group
Minneapolis, Minnesota

Published by Bethany House Publishers
11400 Hampshire Avenue South
Bloomington, Minnesota 55438
www.bethanyhouse.com

Bethany House Publishers is a division of
Baker Publishing Group, Grand Rapids, Michigan

Printed in the United States of America

Library of Congress Cataloging-in-Publication Data
Names: Robinson, Beth, author. | Scott, Latayne C., author.
Title: Protecting your child from predators : how to recognize and respond to sexual danger / Beth Robinson, EdD, Latayne C. Scott, PhD.
Description: Bloomington, Minnesota : Bethany House Publishers, [2019] | Includes bibliographical references.
Identifiers: LCCN 2018059344 | ISBN 9780764233333 (trade paper : alk. paper) | ISBN 9781493418725 (e-book)
Subjects: LCSH: Child sexual abuse—Prevention. | Child sexual abuse—Religious aspects—Christianity. | Parenting—Religious aspects—Christianity.
Classification: LCC HV6570 .R63 2019 | DDC 362.76/7—dc23
LC record available at https://lccn.loc.gov/2018059344

Cover design by Dan Pitts

Authors are represented by Credo Communications, LLC.

19 20 21 22 23 24 25   7 6 5 4 3 2 1

Beth dedicates this book to the courageous children, teens, and parents who have survived and thrived after being sexually abused. Their warrior hearts have inspired her and graced her life.

Latayne dedicates this book to her grandchildren.

Since it is so likely that [our children] will meet cruel enemies, let them at least have heard of brave knights and heroic courage. Otherwise you are making their destiny not brighter but darker.

—C. S. Lewis

Contents

Section III: Ages Twelve and Older

Acknowledgments

The authors would like to gratefully acknowledge the support of their families during this process; the advocacy of Tim Beals, our agent at Credo Communications; and Sam Chan, author of *Evangelism in a Skeptical World*, for his insights about the importance of narratives and scenarios, which so influenced the writing of this book.

Introduction

Creating a Warrior Heart

Is there a parent or grandparent who isn't reeling from the news about the sexual abuse of young people in the sports and entertainment worlds? Is there an educator or church leader who is not grieving—and worried—by what is happening to young children every day?

In the most extreme cases—like that of sports doctor Larry Nassar, who reportedly assaulted more than 150 talented, beautiful young girls[1]—those devastated parents and others in their situation have two questions:

What could I have done to prevent this?

What could I tell other parents that would help them recognize their children are being sexually abused?

If you sit in a pew on Sundays, it's statistically probable that you are surrounded by adults and youth who have been abused but aren't willing or able to talk about it publicly. In fact, my research and experience tell me that on average, 1 in every 4 female churchgoers has been abused in the past, and 1 in 6 of the males.

But it doesn't have to be this way. The past is not the future. This can stop now, and it can stop with the active involvement of parents to inform and protect their children. You can protect your child by empowering him or her to have a warrior heart.

If you are a parent, the birth of your first child automatically made you a protector. Women were gifted with the role of mother, and men were knighted with the privilege of fatherhood. With both roles comes the honor of protecting.

My job as a counselor who specializes in cases involving abused children brings me face-to-face with hurting parents. Someone has injured their innocent child. Somebody has ambushed their lives.

In most cases, the enemy at their gates was not a faceless stranger. The enemy has come inside their gates, has been living there. It was someone they loved and trusted.

In fact, acquaintances or friends are responsible for a full 75 percent of sexual assaults of females.[2]

We would rather think it is the stranger in the trench coat than accept the sickening realization that it was the trusted teacher or the uncle.

While we might reluctantly believe that a predator would groom children, it is even harder to accept that he or she would groom a whole church to gain access to its children. Like Satan, who "masquerades as an angel of light" (2 Corinthians 11:14), he will charm the socks off parents. And the pants off their children.

Just as a predator can have a group as a target, predation itself is often a group project. Entire websites and chat rooms exist where predators give each other advice on how to gain access to children, then boast about and display images of their conquests. This is a giant network hidden from you. You see individual instances popping up like isolated islands in the sea of your experience, in news reports, in whispered stories. But those strategizing criminals live in an intricate web of connectedness beneath the surface.

That weblike structure is not the Internet. It is far, far bigger than that.

This is about cosmic warfare: "*For our struggle is not against flesh and blood, but against the rulers, against the authorities, against the powers of this dark world and against the spiritual forces of evil in the heavenly realms*" (Ephesians 6:12, italics added).

Most people wear blinders about pedophiles because we super-impose our ideas about normal sexual attraction onto abnormal people. Pedophiles are wired differently than we are—they aren't sexually stimulated by the same circumstances as the rest of us. In fact, they are attracted and stimulated in ways that make no sense to us.

We can hardly bring ourselves to believe these shocking statistics:

- Thirty-four percent of child sexual abuse victims are *under* nine years of age; only 26 percent of the child sexual abuse victims are between the ages of twelve and fourteen.[3]

- Research estimates that approximately 1 in 6 boys and 1 in 4 girls are sexually abused before the age of eighteen.[4]

- Although sexual abuse is not uncommon in males, we tend to think only females are at risk.

Furthermore, we believe that *we would certainly know it* if our child had been sexually assaulted. However, up to 40 percent of children who are sexually abused do not exhibit any symptoms.[5]

Even if there are indications of abuse, the signs can be very subtle. When children are trying to disclose abuse, they often only imply that something has happened to them without directly stating that they were sexually abused. They may be testing the reaction of parents or other adults by hinting at rather than stating what has happened. If children believe that a small hint has been accepted well, they may follow with a larger hint.[6]

Children often don't disclose abuse because they are afraid their abuser will harm them or their family members. They often delay making a disclosure until adulthood.[7]

When children do disclose, they generally tell friends or siblings. If they tell a family member other than a sibling, it is usually a mother.

Few children disclose to authorities or professionals. If children do disclose to an authority figure, they usually will tell a teacher.[8]

Males tend not to disclose their victimization, so the abuse of males may be significantly underreported. A male feels societal pressure to be strong and not be seen as a victim.[9]

No book can tackle all the aspects of this problem: its causes, its symptoms, its aftereffects, and solutions for recovery.

When you read this book, the sheer breadth of what evil can do might overwhelm you. I suggest you think of this book as a buffet from which you can select what fits your needs—not as an entire sixteen-course meal. Continue reading the introductory chapters, then choose the scenarios that interest you most. You don't get extra credit for reading the whole book, so relax and learn.

In addition, I have very good news for parents whose children have been affected by sexual abuse. As I look back at decades of cases in which I've counseled children, I can assure you that children are very resilient. With treatment, children can put sexual abuse behind them, especially if it was of short duration and/or occurred fairly early in childhood.

So there is hope in disaster. But this book starts *before* the problems, with information, insights, and strategies.

You have an incredible resource right inside you. It is the grace of God: "It teaches us to say 'No' to ungodliness and worldly passions, and to live self-controlled, upright and godly lives in this present age" (Titus 2:11–12).

Having a warrior heart means learning to say "No" to whatever puts that heart at risk. You have a warrior heart in protecting your child.

And you can create just that kind of brave, noble, and prepared heart in your child. A child's warrior heart takes training. Let's get started.

—Beth Robinson, EdD

1

Know the Turf, Have a Plan, Protect Your Children

Face it, there are an increasing number of situations in daily life that are no longer safe—at least not unless you as a parent put in place the boundaries to keep your children safe in them. You can do this not just by restricting their access to dangerous places and dangerous people, but by helping your children create with you mental and spiritual safety zones where they and you know how to protect them; where they can say with courage and authority, "NO!" This is the essence of empowering the warrior heart of your child.

Jesus told us that we have to live in this world. But we don't have to—indeed we must not—let that world live in us, forcing us to live by its rules and twisted logic, to submit to its perils (John 17:14–15).

And in a Christian worldview where we try to be accepting of sinners while hating the sin, we need to realize that crimes against children are especially hateful to God. They are a special class of sin.

Jesus takes it personally. Whoever welcomes a child, said Jesus, "welcomes me" (Mark 9:37 NET).

But sin against a child? It's better to tie a large rock around a perpetrator's neck and sink him or her in the ocean than to take the innocence of a child. (Don't get mad at me; Jesus said that in Matthew 18:6.)

All your protection of your children has a deeply spiritual basis, one set in place by God himself who alone fully knows the value of every individual He created.

The apostle Paul acknowledged that there is a time to speak as a child, and you as a parent must be ready to communicate at the level of your child's understanding. This book, divided into three parts, will show you what to say and how to say it to

- children under the age of six,
- children ages six to eleven, and
- tweens and teens twelve and older.

For instance, we'll learn how to teach a child under the age of six

- the correct terms for sexual body parts,
- an insistence that their bodies belong to them and that they have a right to say "no" to unwanted touch, and
- when and with whom they can discuss their bodies.

Similarly, we'll learn about how to have protective talks about sexual behaviors with older children as well.

In addition, we will explore everyday scenarios in which abuse can and often does occur. Far from turning you into an overprotective "helicopter parent," I can show you how to give your children the knowledge and skills to protect themselves—so their own awareness is their first line of defense even when you aren't around.

These scenarios, I hope, will remove some of the mystery and allay some of the fears parents have about the procedures that follow disclosure of child sexual abuse. Rest assured that professionals are very sensitive to the distress involved—and to the hope and healing that disclosure and counseling can bring to even dire situations.

There are several main groups of influence from which most sexual abuse comes:

- Authority figures such as teachers, coaches, and ministers
- Close family friends or family members, whether immediate family or extended family
- Peers (other children)
- Strangers
- Technology

"Most of those are people I trust!" you might say. *Exactly.* Trust is the oil that greases the gears of abuse. Without trust, most abuse could never happen.

For each age group, we will look at scenarios from these abuser groups. The only exception is that we will not cover technology for preschool-age children, because preschoolers should not have access to devices connected to the Internet and need to have adult supervision any time they are using technology.

The Geography of the Turf

One essential preparation for what we'll discuss in this book are definitions of sexual abuse of a child. Here are the types:

- Sexual touching—including penetration
- Masturbation between adults and children

- Vaginal or anal intercourse
- Oral/genital contact or sex
- Indecent exposure
- Use of children in pornographic filming or photographs
- Showing children pornographic filming or photographs
- Encouraging or forcing children to witness sexual acts
- Encouraging or forcing children to prostitute themselves

These are the situations I want to help you prevent. There are ways to raise kids and keep them safe in the scenarios of everyday life. I'm not saying that every scenario in this book—going to camp, for instance—is a bad thing. But there are sometimes bad people in good settings like these.

I'm going to invite you into the lives of the normal, average people who fill my case files. Of course, I have protected the anonymity of moms and dads and their kids by changing their names and some details of the situations. But these are people just like you, who would be the first to say, "Use what happened to us to keep it from happening to others."

We will meet parents of children under age six. We will see situations such as daycare, family reunions, small group studies, and playgrounds in which real people's experiences can teach us what to watch for with small children, and how to protect their innocence while keeping others from breaching it.

We will meet parents of children six to eleven in music lessons, summer camp, and walking in their neighborhoods. We'll learn how to start conversations with your children and what red flags to watch for.

Parents of teenagers will share their experience with social media and technology, mission trips, dating situations, and even shopping malls.

Boundaries are good things. Healthy, helpful things. In the Old Testament, one of the worst, most dishonest things you could do was to move the boundary stones between you and your neighbor. What is yours is yours. Your family is yours, and your warrior heart knows that. If your child goes into a situation, you protect what is yours by setting boundaries. You can't let your kids go into any potential danger without having set up boundaries that they understand, and that they can implement and use to their advantage.

This is not a book of scare tactics, but of safety tactics.

This book isn't about how to help people recover from horrible circumstances, though through the grace and healing of God, people can. God has given children incredible resilience and ability to recover from such things. This book, however, focuses on preventing your children from being abused.

Jesus, who slammed adults for criticizing the enthusiasm of children (Matthew 19:13–14), also drew lines to protect them. The innocence and fervency of children are treasures. Jesus is deeply, emotionally involved in the lives of believers and their children.

And He portrays himself in the Bible, over and over again, as the ultimate Warrior, Champion of the innocent.

I want every kid to be carefree. I want children to be kids for as long as they should be kids. But my determination to help them is matched by innumerable people who *don't* want that for your child.

I serve families who have faced the unthinkable. They would say to you, "At the very least, something good can come out of our pain. Our experiences can help someone else." They will become a "cloud of witnesses" whose teachings can help you run this difficult race of parenthood. Let these moms and dads, and let me, help you empower your child's warrior heart by showing you

- how to introduce conversations about sex and safety, even to toddlers;

- where the dangers can lurk;
- how prevalent the dangers are;
- the signs you can look for; and
- how to talk to your kids about these things in a way that will protect them but not scare them to death.

Talk to your child.
Know the turf.
Have a plan.
Keep your kids safe.

2

You Want Me to Talk about Sex?

Sometimes parents, even those who attend church regularly, find it difficult to discuss spiritual matters with their children. Perhaps it's because we feel that a Sunday school teacher or youth leader might have so much more background and preparation than we do. But unless we want our children to grow up thinking there's a "church world" and a "real world" that have little relation to each other, we have to begin talking about God to show He plays an important role in everyday life. (For instance, we might begin with thanking God out loud for good circumstances and finding ways to praise Him in difficult times.)

The same thing is true about talking to children about their bodies and their sexuality. If you want your children to understand the spiritual values that God holds for sexuality, you have to talk to your children about their sexuality. If you don't teach your children about sexual purity and the way they can protect it, rest assured that sooner or later, somebody will. And probably in a way you don't want.

Talking to your children about their bodies, sexuality, and relationships is easiest when they are preschoolers, when the topics are simpler and easier to address. As your children get older, the topics will get more complicated and will be more difficult to have conversations about if you have not started when they are younger. Think about laying groundwork. You can do it. It is not nearly as difficult as you think it will be. Start simple and work your way up to complex.

- *Keep conversations small but regular.* Children don't remember information when we share it one time. The best way to communicate information about sexuality, relationships, and spiritual values is through regular conversations that become a part of daily living. Our children are inundated daily with messages about sexuality through media and their friends. We have to communicate with our children regularly to help them process the information they are getting from other sources.

- *Have a conversation, not a lecture.* Too frequently we lecture our kids instead of having a dialogue with them. When we listen to our children, we learn about the world they are living in. Their perceptions of the world are different from our perceptions, and through back-and-forth conversation, we can assess what they know and don't know.

- As a parent, you should be able to *communicate to your children in three to five sentences any important concepts.* If you use more than three to five sentences, you will have lost your children's attention. If your children want more information than you have provided in those few sentences, they will ask questions. Remember, you are having regular conversations with your children, so you will be able to provide information in manageable increments.

- *When kids ask questions, answer them honestly.* This will help your kids know that they can come to you when they have questions and that you will welcome helping them. If you don't know the answer to a question, be honest and admit you don't know, then do some research to find out the answer for your child. By admitting you don't know something and then finding the answer, you communicate two things to your children. First, your children will know they are important enough for you to spend time researching a question for them. Nothing communicates to our children how important they are more than spending time with them. Second, by searching for answers to questions we don't know, we strengthen our children's trust in our ability to find good solutions for them.

- *Don't react with too much emotion to situations and thus indirectly teach lessons you don't want to teach.* When we are confronted with situations in which our children are saying or doing something that we interpret to be sexual, it's natural initially to have strong emotional reactions. Give yourself a mental time-out to strategize in view of what your emotional reactions will communicate to your children. It is our responsibility to take care of our own emotional reactions rather than inflicting our responses on our children. We teach, not traumatize. A calm response that provides information and direction will instruct our children about healthy sexuality, while an emotional response will shut down communication with our children and hinder the message that our sexuality is a gift from God.

- *Teaching kids about sex is easier when we use teachable moments.* Teachable moments occur when your kids are talking about a topic or see or hear information in the media that will allow you to open up a conversation about spiritual values. Allow your children to talk about their interactions with friends and what they are seeing and hearing on social media. How many times have you been in the car and your children were talking about random or unimportant things? Use such times for teachable moments.

- *If your children don't ask questions, don't pressure them.* Instead, remind your children that you are available to answer questions. Some children are too shy to ask questions. If your children are not willing to ask questions, you don't have to have direct conversations with them; you can use other methods to communicate information about sexuality. For example, you can try having a conversation with your spouse or a good friend and allow your children to overhear it. Children are generally curious about our conversations with other adults, and we can use that curiosity to communicate information our children need to know.

Casual, "bite-sized," spontaneous conversations about important things is not a new concept. In Deuteronomy 11:19, Moses had instructions for parents about teaching important things: "Teach them to your children, talking about them when you sit at home and when you walk along the road, when you lie down and when you get up."

Though those verses refer specifically to teaching God's law to children, it's equally true that important conversations about their bodies and God's role in their lives must be taught the same way.

Teach your children in the morning. Teach your children in the evening. Teach your children in the car. Teach your children during dinner conversations. While waiting for the sitter. On vacation. With your Christian friends who have children who will likewise listen.

Let your fierce, wise protectiveness and love of your family create warrior hearts in them, in young people who will know how to say NO loudly and bravely and insistently against any ungodly person who wishes them harm.

Children Five and Under

3

Children Five and Under

What They Should Know

It may seem obvious that a fifteen-year-old needs different information than a five-year-old. What may not be so obvious is that sex education begins in infancy. We teach our young children a lot of information about their bodies and sexuality before they even learn to talk. By keeping genitals covered, for instance, we demonstrate without words that they are not for display (1 Corinthians 12:23). Certainly by age five, a parent should have taught children about God and His role in their creation. By this time, your children should be comfortable talking with you about God and their bodies.

Here are some things your children should know by age five.

God created your child's body. As we interact with our children on a daily basis, we tell them that God created them in a fearful and wonderful way.

Here are some ways to talk about that:

"Did you know that while you were still inside Mommy, God had already selected just the right nose for you?"

"Did you know you aren't like anybody in the whole world because God used His best imagination to make you extra special?"

(In front of a mirror) "Can you count your hairs? Did you know that God has counted every hair on your head, and He knows when even one comes off in your hairbrush?"

"What foods make your stomach sick? Did you know that God already knew that before you ate it the first time because He made your insides? He knows all about you!"

The concepts of maleness and femaleness. In today's culture, it is essential to show your confidence that God made deliberate decisions with each human body, and you can tell your child that each child has a place on his or her body that tells everyone what decision God made. You can also point out other physical differences:

"Do you know that only women have a special cushy place inside them where a baby can grow?"

"Do men or women usually have beards?"

"Why can't ladies go to the bathroom standing up?"

"What is there about your body that shows that God made you a boy or a girl?"

Correct names for body parts. Because your child will literally be "growing into" his or her body and will eventually have to refer to its parts accurately, he or she should know correct anatomical names. However, just as we have "inside voices" and "outside voices," you might refer in public to your child's "bottom" or "private parts," while insisting that in your home, with family members, the specific terms—such as penis, testicles, anus, vagina, and breasts—be used when specificity is needed. But "private parts" is usually sufficient otherwise.

This may feel awkward for you at first! If you think it will be, practice talking about these terms in front of a mirror as if you are talking to your child. If you feel embarrassed by discussing sexual issues and spiritual values, tell your child so, but continue the discussion. Remember that having discussions about spirituality and sexuality provides you an opportunity to develop a deeper sense of trust between you and your child, and to equip them to make their own godly decisions.

Children can talk to Mom and Dad about their bodies. If you use the strategies discussed in this chapter, your children will understand that they can talk to you about their bodies—which will prepare them to feel comfortable talking to you about sexuality as they get older. Although it may be several years before preschool children's bodies begin to physically change due to puberty, they may have older siblings in the home and notice such changes. Or they may be curious about the private parts of their parents. Make sure they can ask about such changes, or ask about anything that has to do with their own private parts, without being made to feel "naughty" or "dirty." Assure them that your home is a safe place for questions.

The definition of a safe touch. Although being able to identify body parts by their anatomical names is a great goal, most parents are at first more comfortable talking about "private parts." One of the easiest ways to talk about private parts in general is to describe them as the parts of the body covered by a swimming suit.

In addition, children need to recognize the difference between safe and unsafe touches. Safe touches make kids feel safe and calm, like a hug from a parent. Touches that are not safe make kids feel nervous, scared, or uncomfortable.

One of the notable exceptions to a safe touch that might make a child uncomfortable would be in a medical setting. Help your children recognize that when a medical professional is examining them, you should be present.

Using the terms *safe* and *unsafe* helps kids communicate their feelings when they are not safe. Some professionals and parents lean toward using the terms *good touch* and *bad touch*, but the problem with labeling touches as "bad" is that kids will think *they* are being bad if they are touched inappropriately—and won't want to tell adults, because being bad means getting in trouble.

Any time children experience a touch that is not safe, they should immediately tell their parents or other safe adults. Children should be assured, repeatedly, that they will *never* get in trouble for telling parents about touches that are not safe.

One tool that I have developed for conversations with young children is my *Safe Touch* line of coloring books. These allow for discussions of people and scenarios in a way that is low pressure for both child and parents.

Demonstrate and role-play the difference between a secret and a surprise. Children need to know that keeping secrets from their parents is never okay. However, it is important to explain the difference between surprises and secrets. *Surprises* are something parents may not know about for a short period of time, but when parents find out they will be happy. Surprises are things like Christmas gifts and birthday parties. *Secrets* are things parents don't know about, things children are told not to share with parents. When parents find out about secrets, they will be sad or angry, not happy. You can practice and role-play secrets and surprises. Just make sure you supervise the secrets part of the conversation so as not to let the child's imagination run the show. Some examples you could use in role-playing a secret might be when a child has eaten forbidden cookies and doesn't say so, or when a child breaks a vase in the house and doesn't tell you. Try not to make the secret scary in the role-playing and discussion.

Talk about situations in which a child shouldn't obey an older person. The structure of authority—especially as taught in Ephesians and elsewhere where God demonstrates that everyone has some authority to which they must yield—is in most cases good and wholesome and orderly. Children need to know, though, that there are times when they should not do what adults tell them to do. Explain that if adults ask them to do something that is not safe or makes them feel uncomfortable, they should (1) leave the situation and (2) tell you as quickly as possible.

Role-play and describe to your children circumstances in which children should not obey adults. (For instance, if any person of any age wants to talk about—or touch them on—parts of their bodies that a bathing suit would cover.) Discuss with them what it means to leave a situation, act it out, and express fervently that you will always listen to them and love them no matter what has happened.

Identify people your children should tell if they are not safe. Obviously, we want to be the first ones our children turn to if they are not safe. However, there may be times when they need to tell other people. Teach your children to tell their teachers, police officers, and medical personnel if they do not feel safe. Emphasize that they must *keep telling adults* until they are safe. If telling one adult does not help them get safe, they need to tell another adult and another adult until they are. Tell the child he has a warrior heart that boldly speaks the truth, and someone will eventually listen, whether the situation is one of physical or sexual safety.

The decisions of a warrior heart. The core goal of all of these conversations and strategies is to transfer from your heart to your child's heart a fierce sense of protectiveness of his or her sexuality. Sexuality is a gift from God, not an accident or just a means to further the human race. This gift has tremendous value and tremendous risks that no child can possibly comprehend. But they can comprehend your love and passion for protecting them.

You can do this!

Here are some prompts: "God created your body with extra special care —it's not like anyone else's in the world. And He also gave you a special brain! How can you use that brain to make sure you talk about your private parts only at home or with Mommy and Daddy?" (At this point, role-play a child's responses such as, "No! I don't talk about those things!" or, "No! My mommy and daddy love me and they say you can't touch me there!" or, "I am going to tell my mom and dad because they want to hear about things like this!")

Finally, don't be too hard on yourself. As you read through this book, recognize that you are learning new skills. Our culture has changed drastically, and our children are coping with this information at younger ages than we did.

You will make mistakes and you will learn. Making mistakes is better than not addressing sexual and spiritual issues. Remember, failure is the greatest teacher. Your children will survive your mistakes and you will develop a healthy, intimate relationship with them as well.

In the next four chapters, we will explore situations in which your children may be at risk for sexual exploitation. We will present seemingly benign situations and the risks they present to your children, and we'll help you recognize the risks. In addition, each chapter will give you practical strategies to create a warrior heart, to help your children prepare for the situations, and to know how to react if they are in danger.

4

Abuse by Authority Figure
The Sitter

A s I enter my office, I see a too-familiar sight: A thin woman with wavy brown hair sits curled in a chair. I heard her sobs even before I opened the door.

I hadn't met Heather before, but from the records waiting on my desk, I knew that she needed tissues and time to cry. Eventually, her sobs get quieter. She glances toward another door across the hallway, where through a window she can see her four-year-old son, David, a ball of toddler energy with multiple cowlicks, tossing a foam ball with one of my interns.

Then Heather wads up a pile of used tissues and carries them to the trash can. With that action, she seems to put away her tears to focus on providing me with information.

This wasn't the first time she had to tell this story. Earlier at a care center, trained sexual assault nurse examiners had gently examined little David. With kind words and soothing actions, they gathered forensic evidence for the coming prosecution of child abuse.

No, Heather had not harmed her child. Her baby-sitter and the sitter's boyfriend had.

"I'm sorry to have to ask you these questions," I say as Heather slowly meets my eyes, "but the information you provide will be helpful as I work with David."

Heather nods. "He was waking up at night complaining that his bottom and his private parts hurt. He would have trouble going back to sleep and told me about bad dreams he kept having."

I nod.

"So I checked for a rash or bruising and I didn't see anything. I was at my wits' end. So I took him in to his pediatrician, thinking he must have an infection or something. I was surprised when the doctor and his nurse asked me to leave the room when they were examining him, but I understand why now."

I already know what the doctor discovered. I offer, "David didn't want to tell the doctor either."

Heather gives me a look of surprise and then relief.

"No, David told the doctor it was a secret." She seems to be having trouble holding her composure, and I offer more tissues but she shakes her head and continues.

The doctor assured David that he wanted to protect him, that it was his job to know about all the parts of children, including the private parts, and if anyone had been hurting him. Gradually David began to tell his story. The baby-sitter, Maria, and her boyfriend had made a "game" out of touching David's genitals and having him touch theirs. To assure his compliance, they told David that if he told what they'd been doing, they would take him away from his mom and he would never see her again.

"The doctor put a halt to that thinking," Heather says. "He told David the game was wrong, and that if they even tried to take him away, they could be put in jail."

Smart doctor, I thought.

"He also told David that it wasn't his fault that Maria and her boyfriend made him play those games. He wasn't in trouble. In fact, he was being very brave to tell about this." She draws herself up in the chair. "And you know what, after the doctor told me what had been going on and I went into the room where David was, David wanted to protect me! He said, 'Momma, don't cry!'

"But I can't get over the fact that I hadn't kept him safe." She begins to cry again. "I can't believe I hired someone who abused my son. How could I do that to him?"

I put my hand over her wrist and speak firmly.

"You didn't do this to him. Maria and her boyfriend hurt David, not you. When you thought David was hurt, you took him to the doctor. You didn't know what was happening to him. You did the best you could to keep him safe."

Heather drops her head. "Will David ever be okay?"

I knew I had a truthful answer from years of experience that would comfort her.

"David will be okay. I'll work with him so that he will feel safe again."

While I know that David will indeed be all right, I wish that his mother had been more aware of ways to select and monitor her baby-sitter. Every parent needs to be aware of ways to select daycares, nannies, and baby-sitters.

Hiring Your Child's Caregivers

It is your job to screen any in-home caregivers thoroughly during the hiring process to help keep your children safe. You want someone who shares your ideas about how to raise children. (While screening involves more than just checking for safety, this book only addresses screening for safety.)

41

Generally, the safest place to begin is by networking through friends and family members. Extend your search to your church and parachurch organizations that might refer capable applicants. If you cannot find a good applicant from your personal networking, consider organizations such as International Nanny Association (www.nanny.org) or www.eNannySource.com.

Interviewing Prospective Caregivers

When you find a suitable candidate, always meet face-to-face. Ask questions like these:

- Tell us about your work with children.
- Why did you decide to become a baby-sitter or nanny?
- What are some of your favorite activities to do with children?
- What do you do when a child has a temper tantrum?
- What type of discipline techniques have you used?
- How would you handle a situation in which a child fell and broke her arm?

Take notes about the applicants' responses and your gut instinct about each candidate.

Do Your Own Social Media Background Check

Next, conduct a social media background check. A quick look at social media posts on Facebook, Instagram, Twitter, and other social media sites will give you a good sense of what the applicant is like. While you can only search the public profile of applicants, in many cases this will give you a good idea of the interests and values of the applicant. Make notes about any posts that concern you. Look for posts that

- violate the values you want your child's caregiver to demonstrate,
- show recklessness or poor judgment,
- indicate substance use, or
- demonstrate aggression.

Focus on what the candidate posts, not what other people post on the applicant's social media site. The applicant may have friends or relatives who don't share the applicant's values, and it's not fair to judge them by the comments of those people. However, if the applicant closely associates with people who don't share your values, you will need to consider if the applicant will allow your children to have contact with their friends and family. Ideally, applicants would have the maturity to remove any inappropriate social media posts from friends and family. If you find red flags, you may want to give the applicant a chance to explain the posts if they end up being your only concern about him or her.

As a general rule, I don't recommend using a third party to do your social media background checks. Most sites that provide these checks are geared toward the business world and don't screen for all the types of issues for parents.

Check References Thoroughly

If your candidate comes from an agency, don't depend on the agency's background check. Agencies get paid when they place applicants, thus they have a vested interest in "helping" you choose one of their applicants.

Ask the applicant for a list of previous employers, then call them and ask some of the following questions:

- What did you like about the applicant?
- What would you change about the applicant?
- What are your children's ages?
- What type of activities did the applicant do with your children?
- How did the applicant respond to your directions as an employer?
- Were there ever situations in which you felt uncomfortable about the decisions the applicant made?
- Why did the applicant leave?
- Would you hire the applicant again?

In addition to interviewing previous employers, ask the applicant if he or she has ever been investigated for child abuse. Conduct your own criminal background check using online services. If you're not sure how to do this, the International Nanny Association lists members who will conduct nanny background checks. Make sure the candidate knows that you are going to conduct the background check and get their signature on a statement authorizing you to do so. Most states require consent from a job applicant to conduct a background check.

Many parents don't think to check an applicant's driving record, but this is essential if a sitter is going to be driving with your children in the car.

Teenage Baby-Sitters

It's a fact that teenagers today are not growing up with the same responsibilities and expectations that existed when I was a child (back when there were dinosaurs in my backyard). We know that teenagers' social and emotional development is progressing more slowly: A college freshman today has the social and emotional development that a high school freshman had twenty years ago.[1]

Second, teenagers today, as a general rule, live on their phones. I have concerns about a teenager being able to focus on watching children without interference from technology. (Actually, I have the same concern for many adults.) Teens don't have the life experience to anticipate what might happen that would keep a child from being safe.

Third, teens tend to be influenced by their peers and might have a hard time saying no to friends who want to come hang out with them while they are baby-sitting. I don't want to hire a baby-sitter who will open my house up for other teenagers.

Finally, what if the teenager you hire is being victimized by a sexual predator? If a teenager can't protect himself or herself from sexual assault, he or she may not be able to protect your child.

While I can't make a decision for other parents about using teenagers as baby-sitters, I would discourage it as a general rule.

However, we all know there are exceptional teens who would make responsible baby-sitters. These teens will have training about baby-sitting and will be certified in CPR. In addition, they will meet the same standards as other baby-sitters or nannies.

Define Your Expectations for Your Child's Caregiver

- Once you're confident you have a suitable caregiver, tell the sitter directly that you expect him or her to be interacting with your child rather than being on a phone or the Internet except for emergencies. (This is a job, after all, not a favor they are doing you.)

- Instruct the caregiver to limit the screen time for your children, specifying what types of media content are appropriate for your children. (One aspect of sexual safety is to protect your child from exposure to pornographic images or content.)

- Insist that anyone else coming into your home or being introduced to your child through the caregiver must have your *prior approval*. In general, you don't want a caregiver inviting peers or relatives over to your house. (Whether they're interacting with the sitter, or worse, with your child, they shouldn't be there.)

- Discuss dressing and toileting of your young children. Tell the caregiver if your children can dress and toilet themselves, and ask that the sitter not "help" children who can do this themselves. You should be concerned if a caregiver is involved in toileting activities or bathing of children who do not require help from the care provider.

Listen and Watch How Your Child Responds

Before hiring an in-home caregiver for your child, assess how your child responds to the caregiver. Introduce the caregiver to your child and allow your child and the caregiver time to play together and get to know one another. Once the caregiver leaves, allow your child to tell you what he or she thinks about the caregiver. This is a perfect opportunity to follow up on previous discussions and reaffirm that you trust your child and will always listen to him or her.

Selecting a Daycare for Your Children

While the logistics of selecting a daycare are slightly different, the same safety elements need to be addressed. Here are some suggestions.

- *Read the online reviews of the daycare.* Any business may have an occasional negative review, but you should be concerned if you see a pattern of negative reviews.
- *Tour the daycare facility.* As you walk around, check for placement of cameras and monitoring of children. You should be concerned if you see children who are not being monitored by adults or if you see adults isolated one-on-one with children where other people cannot see them. Ask about the types of background checks and screening the daycare conducts for employees.
- *Ask about the facility's policies on who may come into the daycare and have contact with the children.* Many facilities have janitors or bus drivers—have they undergone background checks? If the daycare is run in a home or by a family, other family members may be there—have they undergone background checks?

Pay attention to warning signs. There are some distinct red flags in daycare facilities that you should be aware of. These red flags include:

- Parents are not encouraged or even allowed to visit during the day.
- There are restricted areas where parents are not allowed in the daycare.
- Children are left without direct adult supervision.

- One teacher is with more children than he or she can manage.
- Caregivers are demeaning or yelling at children.
- Children are playing roughly with each other and adults are not redirecting them.

After you have toured a facility, take your child to see it. Let your child interact with the caregiver he or she will be spending most of their time with at the daycare, and pay attention to your child's reaction to the facility and the caregiver.

Monitoring Your Child's Caregivers

No matter how much effort you spend selecting a daycare, nanny, or baby-sitter, it is equally important to monitor your child's caregivers after you hire them. There are several ways to check up on how your child is adjusting to the caregiver situation.

First, talk to your children and listen carefully to their responses about the caregivers. What were the activities of the day? What games did your child play? What was different about today than other days? Mentally note if your child mentions meeting someone new or talks about an activity that is new or different. Playfully ask questions every day about what they did. As you talk to your children, always tell them you want to keep them safe and that they will not be in trouble for telling you about their day.

If your children are not old enough to talk, you can play games with your children that can help you know what is going on during the day. For example, if your child is in daycare, you can play school with your child. You play the role of the child and have your child tell you what to do. In this way, your child can express what is going on during the day.

If your children complain about caregivers, follow up with your children's caregivers and ask for an explanation of situations leading to complaints. Just asking questions about the caregiver's behaviors may lead to caregivers changing their behaviors before the behaviors become dangerous.

Use a Camera

Regardless of whether you take your child to a daycare or hire an in-home caregiver, you should monitor your child's caregivers with a camera. Any reputable daycare will have cameras installed throughout the facility. When you place a child in a daycare facility, walk through the facility and make sure there are no areas without a camera. Make sure the camera coverage is accessible to you via a web-based platform, such as one on your phone. You also need to have a copy of your child's schedule and be able to log in throughout the day and make sure your child is in the room where he or she is scheduled to be.

If your child is at home, buy a security camera. There are inexpensive models under $50 that are simple to set up. While your child is in the care of a nanny or baby-sitter, check in regularly on your cell phone to monitor what is happening in your home. Tell your caregivers upfront that you will be monitoring them with cameras, and they should be comfortable with this. If your caregiver is regularly offscreen or if your camera system goes offline, you need to be concerned.

Practice Intrusive Supervision

Whether your children are at a daycare, at a friend's house, or at home, you need to provide intrusive supervision: You go where your children are, and put eyes on your children. Clearly, I think using technology is important, but technology can be manipulated. If you arbitrarily drop in on your child at home or at a daycare, you send a message to your caregivers that you are serious about your child's care. If you are at work, use your lunch hour at random times to check on your child. You will find out what activities your child is doing and whether they are spending time just sitting around watching TV. Alternately, if you can't physically drop in, make a phone call and ask questions about what your children are doing and ask to speak to them.

Pay Attention to How Other People React to Your Child's Caregivers

When you run into the lifeguard at the local pool and she says how amazing your baby-sitter is and she loves how happy your children are this summer, you have positive feedback. On the other hand, if you run into the lifeguard and she comments on how your baby-sitter really loves being on her cell phone, you have feedback that should concern you. While casual acquaintances or even good friends may not come right out and say that your baby-sitter worries them, they will often have a revealing reaction. For instance, a neighbor may casually mention that there was an extra car parked at your house this week.

Keep Up with Social Media

Vetting your caregiver through social media isn't just for the application phase. Set aside regular time to observe online what goes on in a caregiver's life. If your caregiver's posts make you uncomfortable, talk with him or her. In addition, you need to monitor social media sites to make sure that your child's caregiver is not posting pictures of your child on social media. Under no circumstances should your child's caregivers post pictures of your child online.

Run a Background Check Once a Year

People's life circumstances change. If you employ a caregiver for more than a year, you should run another background check. Let your child's caregiver know you are running a background check again and have him or her sign a new release. You should be as thorough and discriminating in the second background check as you are in the first one.

Special Note on Infant Abuse

I recently got a heartbreaking note from a mother. "There are signs I look back on with my daughter's abuse as a baby under one year old that now make sense to me [indicating] that there was probably ongoing abuse at the time," she wrote.

The reality is that some predators are attracted to infants. While you never want to believe that your infant could be sexually abused, you need to pay attention to signs of sexual abuse in infants. The most obvious signs will be physical and will include bruises, bleeding, or rashes in the genital area, venereal disease, difficulty with bowel movements, or stained and bloody diapers. In addition, you may notice changes in your child's eating and sleeping patterns, and your baby may become difficult to soothe and may seem irritable all the time. Your child might consistently scream and cry when one person enters the room and not respond this way to other people. In combination with the other symptoms, your child might begin to self-stimulate.

Trust Your Instincts

The most important thing you can do is trust your instincts. Parenting is a sacred job. Christian parents have the Holy Spirit indwelling, and one of His functions is to guide people into truth. Trust yourself! Your instincts about your child's safety are generally accurate. Ask questions about what's troubling you, and don't take vague answers from a caregiver. If something feels wrong to you, follow up, check up, verify.

Messages for Your Child

(The following information, with changes appropriate to different age groups, will appear at the end of each upcoming chapter.)

Keep nurturing that warrior heart. Kids can learn to safeguard themselves if you give them the tools. Keep telling them these protective truths:

1. Children have the right to say no to anyone who asks them to do anything painful, embarrassing, or wrong.

2. No one can touch them on the parts of the body covered by a bathing suit, and they should not touch anyone else in these private places.

3. They must tell you immediately if someone tells them to keep a secret or tries to threaten them or bribe them. Assure them repeatedly that you will always be glad to know that, and that they will not be in trouble.

4. If they find themselves alone with an adult or peer in an isolated area where others cannot see them or in an unfamiliar place, they need to leave the situation immediately.

If You Suspect Abuse

There are warning signs of abuse that your child may display, but *remember not all children who are being sexually abused show these signs.* These red flags are when children

1. have physical injuries or have concerns about their genitalia;
2. display an unprecedented shyness about getting undressed in front of others;
3. express an unusual interest in sexual subjects or completely avoid sexual topics;
4. avoid individuals for no apparent reason or don't want to participate in certain activities;
5. experience sleep disturbances, bedwetting, or soiling; or
6. isolate themselves, are depressed, and have suicidal thoughts.

While these are all symptoms of sexual abuse, no single symptom will confirm a child has been sexually abused. If your child is exhibiting one or more of these symptoms, talk with him or her to make sure your child has not been abused.

If you suspect your child has been sexually or physically abused, remember not to overreact emotionally in front of your child. Let the child know that you want to keep him or her safe—that it's your job, and you want to do it.

Take your concerns to a doctor, a social worker, or the police. You don't have to *know* that your child is not safe, you just have to suspect it to seek out professional assistance. And of course, don't leave your child with the caregiver or at the daycare until you're convinced it's safe.

5

Abuse by a Peer

The Small Group Bible Study

When I answered the phone in my office one Thursday morning, I had no idea how it would change my life and ministry.

"Dr. Robinson, this is John Thompson, and we have some mutual friends," he began, giving their names. "Do you have a few minutes?"

I checked and saw that I didn't have any appointments, even though my office hours at the university were usually scheduled full. "Sure," I said.

"I'm an elder at your friends' church, and last night I met with our other elders because of a very difficult situation." He hesitated. "In fact, we're way over our heads with this."

John described a small group of young couples with children who met every Sunday night, rotating between different homes. After a potluck, the adults in the group would stay in the living room for their Bible study while the children played in another room. The kids seemed to play quietly, and it was easier to have the Bible study without the distraction of children in the room.

"But last week, a three-year-old in the group told his mother that he didn't want to go to the small group because he didn't like the games that the other kids were playing when they were in the other room. When the mother asked her son about the game, her son said . . ." John was having difficulty with this next part. "He said that an eight-year-old boy was touching his private parts. At first, the mother couldn't believe what her son was telling her and questioned him again. But she began to freak out when her son was consistent in his description of the game."

As reality dawned on the mother, she became angry. She and her husband called the minister at the church and set an appointment to see him the next morning. At their meeting, the minister wisely encouraged the couple to call Child Protective Services and then told them that he wanted to talk with the elders of the church to see what they needed to do to inform the other parents in the small group.

"We elders decided to call each of the families in the study and let them know what the three-year-old had reported and that CPS had been informed. In the next few days, CPS interviewed all the children. They discovered that the eight-year-old had sexually abused several other children in the group too."

"How did the other parents react to this situation?"

"All over the map, really," John said. "Some were angry, some were sad, some felt guilty and blamed themselves for not knowing. Some of them blamed the parents of the eight-year-old, even blamed the church."

"How can I help?"

"This has torn our church up," John said. "Could you travel over here next weekend and meet with the parents as a group, and individually, and help them cope with the situation?"

Although I had never met with an entire group of parents who had children abused in the same situation, I shuffled my schedule to travel the next weekend to this church in the Bible Belt. After meeting with the minister on Friday night to get his take on how the families were coping, I met on Saturday with each of the couples individually who wanted to come. Then I met with the entire group. It was indeed a spectrum of reactions and emotions. I worked with the parents to help them understand that their children would heal and move on with the right support and counseling. I also tried to help the parents navigate through their guilt and help them understand what they could do in the future to make sure their children were safe.

On Sunday, I sat down with the parents of the eight-year-old who had engaged the younger children in the group in sexual behavior. The parents were devastated. Through this process, they'd learned that their son had been previously sexually abused before he began sexually abusing younger children. The parents felt double guilt and felt isolated in their suffering and confusion.

My last meeting that weekend was with the elders of the church. We discussed ways they could support the families financially, spiritually, and emotionally. As I'll discuss later in this book, many spiritual factors such as forgiveness were at the forefront, and have to be an integral part of any such scenario.

This situation had a profound effect on me. I went back several months later to follow up with the families to see how they were doing and discuss any concerns they had. But I couldn't get out of my mind something the parents told me: They wished they had been able to feel comfortable talking to even their young children about sexual safety before the abuse situation arose.

The parents needed a tool that would assist them in discussing sexual safety. In response to their request, I created a coloring book, *God Made Me: The Safe Touch Coloring Book*, to explain sexual safety in a nonthreatening and conversational way to young children.

While this was my first experience working with a situation in which multiple children were abused in a single setting, I regret to say it was not my last: I have helped numerous churches navigate similar situations.

I'm pleased to say, though, that the children who were abused are doing very well today.

Not a Child

It's hard for any parent to accept the fact that another child may pose a danger to their children. We want to believe that children are innocent. Our idea of who will sexually abuse a child is a man in a dark trench coat, but the reality is very different. Child molesters aren't necessarily socially inept drifters who can be identified as posing a threat to children. In a church or parachurch organization, sexual molesters may be captivating leaders: ministers, Bible teachers, youth leaders, camp counselors, or mission team leaders. Operating under the radar, so to speak, volunteers commit 50 percent of the sexual offenses in churches, while paid staff members commit 30 percent of the offenses, according to research.

As many as 40 percent of children who are sexually abused are abused by older or more powerful children. That means, when you look at your circle of trust, don't forget to include children when you think of both potential perpetrators and potential allies to help you protect your child.[1]

Why Does It Happen?

Christians generally operate on underlying beliefs about the people in the pews next to us. We assume that individuals attending church have good motives and values similar to ours. We want to believe in the good that exists in people, especially if they're in church with us. As a result, we grant familiar people access to our children, access we would never grant a stranger. Because we are so trusting, sexual predators tend to gravitate toward churches because we allow them access to our children.

Here are some reasons this is true:

1. *Closed doors.* The structure of church activities frequently provides open access to sexual offenders. In many churches, one person may teach a children's class behind closed doors. In addition, there may be several church activities running concurrently, which makes it more difficult to directly supervise children and the adults who work with them.

2. *Need for volunteers.* Since churches frequently have difficulty finding volunteers to teach classes and supervise children's activities, any willing person is welcomed with open arms. Unfortunately, some churches still do not screen employees or volunteers who work with youth. Relative newcomers to the church, who for all practical purposes are strangers, are embraced and often put to work immediately with children, without any investigation into their backgrounds.

3. *Lack of criticism.* In trying to maintain a Christian attitude, we might think it's picky or critical to ask questions about how a worker interacts with our children. Even worse, sometimes if we do voice questions or concerns about another person's behavior, church leadership may ignore allegations rather than question someone's conduct, character, or motive.

4. *"It won't happen here."* We want to feel safe, and we see church as a refuge, a safe place of friends, brothers, and

fellow strivers. Unknowingly, church members buy into the belief that a person with dangerous or evil intentions wouldn't prey upon a church because it is sacred. The naïve trust in the institution is exactly what attracts sexual offenders.

5. *"Not one of our own."* In addition, we buy into the myth that a person who appears to be an effective spiritual leader won't engage in inappropriate sexual contact with children. The reality is that a sexual offender may have exceptional social skills that invite other people to trust him. One of the reasons sexual offenders can victimize so many people is because they usually seem like the last person who would hurt a child or teen.

Church Safety Programs

As a parent, you should require that your church have a child safety program—one that provides written and enforced guidelines to keep your child safe in activities at church and offsite at church events. If your church can't or won't provide safeguards for your children, you should seriously consider attending somewhere else.

Some features your church's safety program should include:

- A minimum of two adults should be involved in supervising all church activities attended by children or youth. These adults must have background checks. Even with background checks, lack of evidence of abuse doesn't mean a person is above suspicion. Most predators offend many times before they are accused, much less prosecuted and convicted. But the knowledge that they will have to undergo a background check can often discourage predators from trying to access children at your church, because predators can find another church without such safeguards.

- New volunteers should be paired with experienced teachers for the first six months they are working in the program. Supervision by two adults should be provided until every child is in the custody of a parent or legal guardian. If someone who is not a legal guardian is picking up a child, the volunteer or staff member needs written notification from parents indicating that they can release the child into someone else's custody.

- To be considered for one of the two adults supervising any activity, an individual should be at least twenty-one years of age. Many churches utilize college students as interns and volunteers in their programs. However, as a general rule, college students should not be considered as adult supervisors for most activities. Trust me, I've been a college professor and counselor for many years, and I assure you that college students of today don't necessarily have the life experience to always make good supervision decisions.

- When transporting children as part of a church activity, two adults should ride in every vehicle. If volunteers or staff members are transporting children, they need to have written permission to transport. If workers have to stop a vehicle in a non-public area for any reason while transporting children, they must immediately call in a report of the situation to their immediate supervisor at church. In addition, they should document the events in writing, in case questions concerning the situation arise later.

- Children's activities and classes must be conducted in rooms with windows to the hallway, or the doors of the rooms propped open. Church leaders, ministers, and parents should be able to walk by any class or activity and clearly see what is happening inside the room. Leaders should be encouraged to regularly visit children's activities to encourage and support volunteers. Having an adult regularly monitor the halls and premises during children's activities will help prevent children from wandering off by themselves and will help prevent unknown individuals from accessing the building.

- When children need diapers changed, the changing area should be visible to other adults. An adult should never change a child's diaper in a room alone. Similarly, when children need to go to the bathroom, two adults should accompany the children to the bathroom.

I do understand that staffing Bible classes and church activities to provide a safe environment takes a lot of staff and volunteers. But our children's safety is worth all the extra work.

Church Activities Off-Site

The guidelines above get more difficult to implement when the activities are away from a church building. This requires planning and strategies. Here are some things to consider about safety:

Eyes on children. No matter what the activities your children are involved in, there should be competent, trustworthy adults who are supervising the children, people who acknowledge and accept their responsibility for supervision. In the small group scenario at the beginning of the chapter, adults should have been supervising the children in the other room.

Random intrusive supervision. In addition to having adults supervise children in activities, parents should randomly drop in and check on how children are doing. During a Bible study or other activity, you can leave your class and unobtrusively look through the window or door to see what they are doing and whether they are safe.

Say no. If there are church-related activities where there is not adequate supervision for your children, say no to participating in the activities. Even if you would enjoy the activities, don't risk your child's safety for your social life. Work with your friends and other church members to change the way activities are planned so that children will be safe.

Talk to your children. Prepare your children for any activities they will participate in. Explain what will happen and who will be supervising the activity. Be sure your child knows where you will be and what you will be doing. In addition, remember to always make sure your children know that inappropriate sexual activities are not okay. Use the *Safe Touch Coloring Book* with your children so they know what safe and unsafe touches are.

Messages for Your Child

Keep nurturing that warrior heart. Kids can learn to safeguard themselves if you give them the tools. Keep telling them these protective truths:

1. Children have the right to say no to anyone who asks them to do anything painful, embarrassing, or wrong.
2. No one can touch them on the parts of the body covered by a bathing suit, and they should not touch anyone else in these private places.
3. They must tell you immediately if someone tells them to keep a secret or tries to threaten them or bribe them.

Assure them repeatedly that you will always be glad to know that, and they will not be in trouble.

4. If they find themselves alone with an adult or peer in an isolated area where others cannot see them or in an unfamiliar place, they need to leave the situation immediately.

If You Suspect Abuse

There are warning signs of abuse that your child may display, but *remember not all children who are being sexually abused will have these signs.* These red flags are when children

1. have physical injuries or have concerns about their genitalia;
2. display an unprecedented shyness about getting undressed in front of others;
3. express an unusual interest in sexual subjects or completely avoid sexual topics;
4. avoid individuals for no apparent reason or don't want to participate in certain activities;
5. experience sleep disturbances, bedwetting or soiling; or
6. isolate themselves, are depressed, and have suicidal thoughts.

While these are all symptoms of sexual abuse, no single symptom will confirm a child has been sexually abused. If your child is exhibiting one or more of these symptoms, talk with him or her to make sure your child has not been abused.

If you suspect your child has been sexually or physically abused, remember not to overreact emotionally in front of your child. Let the child know you want to keep him or her safe—that it's your job, and you want to do it.

Take your concerns to a doctor, a social worker, or the police. You don't have to *know* that your child is not safe, you just have to suspect it to seek out professional assistance. And of course, don't leave your child in the same situation if you are concerned about his or her safety.

6

Abuse by Family Member or Trusted Friend

The Cousin

I was not quite sure why Amber, a freshman at the university where I teach, had emailed me a week ago to set up an appointment. She's not one of my students, and I responded that I couldn't do counseling with undergrad students—it would be a conflict of interest. She wrote back that this wasn't for a counseling session but that it was important.

She sits before me. Her clothes—jeans and a T-shirt—are casual, but her pretty, freckled face shows tension. After our self-introductions she sits down, not meeting my eyes, and plays with a fidget toy on my desk.

"Amber, what can I do to help you?"

"I heard that you work with kids who have been sexually abused, and I wanted to talk to you about something that happened to me."

"Since I don't do counseling with undergrad students, do you need me to help you get help through the student counseling center here at the university? It's free."

"I've been to counselors, and they helped. But I came here to tell you what happened so that maybe you can keep it from happening to other kids."

I sit back, a signal that I'm listening.

"My friend Sarah, who is in your class, says that you talk to parents and kids about sexual abuse. Something bad happened to me, but I think I'm doing better than my parents are doing. They blame themselves and can't deal with everything that has happened to the family."

I nod. "Yes, parents can take things really hard. But let's talk about you, first. Does what happened to you cause you to have nightmares or flashbacks?"

She shrugs. "Only occasionally. I used to have lots of nightmares but not anymore."

"Do you think that talking to me will cause you to have nightmares or cause any other problems for you?"

"Actually, no," she says. "I've told other people, and if this helps keep other little kids safe, I don't mind telling it again to someone who can make a difference."

"I'd be honored to listen and use what you tell me to help kids."

She settles back and begins to describe a wonderful childhood in Tennessee with an extended family. She and her sister went with their family on summer trips to see grandparents who lived several hours away. Amber tells me about how she learned to love all kinds of flowers because of the greenhouse her grandmother had behind their house, one that brought extra income to the family because of some of the exotic plants she grew.

"All that changed when my Uncle Michael lost his job, and he and his family moved in with my grandparents. I was five years old, and at first it was so fun to have cousins to play with. We all had chores, to help with the plants, but when they were done we'd play outside all day and watch movies in the basement at night, and it was just a kid's dream. I was the youngest of the cousins, and I always wanted to do what they were doing."

She tips her head to one side, and a cloud passes over her face.

"The oldest of the cousins was Seth, and he was thirteen. One day he was doing chores and went to the greenhouse, and I followed him. He asked if I'd like to play a game, and he told me he had candy in one of his pockets and I should try to find it. It was fun the first few times—what kid doesn't like candy? And all the adults thought it was so cute that the youngest and the oldest both liked going to the greenhouse."

I nod. "But the game changed?"

She looks at me sharply. "Yes, he started hiding candy down the front of his pants and wouldn't give it to me unless I fondled him." She shudders and then continues. "Then I couldn't get candy unless he ejaculated. And then . . . he wanted us to have sex. There was no more candy, just threats unless I did what he said."

I wait.

"I didn't want to go to the greenhouse anymore, but he was really sneaky and would outsmart me and catch me alone, in a bathroom or the basement. When our family went home, I would beg my mom not to take us back to Grandmother's. Sometimes I even faked illness to avoid going. But we went back anyhow."

She wipes away tears. "One day my mom walked into the greenhouse and caught Seth on top of me with his pants down. Mom freaked out. She yelled at Seth and threatened him with a shovel. Seth backed off and apologized. My mom grabbed me and took me up to my grandparents' house. She told my grandparents and my aunt and uncle. They didn't believe that Seth was forcing me to have sex. They argued with my mom and told her that she was confused about what she had seen. Seth made up some story about urinating and losing his balance and falling on top of me.

"My mom reported the abuse to the local sheriff's office. Seth had to go to treatment, but he came home a year later and my grandparents and Uncle Michael's family still don't believe that Seth was sexually abusing me. My mom's side of the family has disowned us and we don't go to visit my grandparents anymore."

Heather squeezes the fidget toy in anger and then asks, "Can you believe that Seth is the one who did something wrong, and my mom and my family are the ones getting punished?"

A Situation That's Hard to Accept

Perhaps no other scenario of sexual abuse has such ability to stab to the core of the warrior heart of a parent as does abuse by a close relative. When a perpetrator is a stranger or distant acquaintance, we know how to feel: us against them. When the perpetrator is family, it is a matter of blood and heritage, of deepest feelings of betrayal, of ripped-apart loyalties, of an uncharted nightmarish future filled with ongoing decisions.

No wonder nice, normal people who discover family sexual abuse often want to cover it up. Not only is the discovery horrific, the implications of reporting it to police can be an unbearable choice. Who is blamed? Who gets punished? Can you stop it in-house, literally, and make sure it never happens again? But if you do that, how can you get help for the child who was molested?

When sexual abuse occurs between cousins, siblings, or step-siblings, the abuse is often hidden from relatives, friends, neighbors, and the community at large. It is the stuff of horrible reality shows, shrouded in secrecy, threats, and social stigma.

Incest, particularly incest involving children and adolescents, is not only underreported and under-recognized, it often goes unpunished. Sibling abuse specifically is the least recognized form of incest, according to experts who have researched it. In fact, sibling incest may occur five times as frequently as parent-child sexual abuse.

Studies show that children often suffer in silence for years when the abuser is a relative who is a minor. Intimidation is often a factor. And one of the biggest problems is that many children do not see themselves as victims of sibling incest, and many families and professionals fail to recognize the abuse.

A False Sense of Security

Recognizing the reality and prevalence of sexual abuse by relatives, Latayne has written a novella for teens, *The Mona Lisa Mirror Mystery* (Cruciform Press, 2018), that deals with this situation. Told from the point of view of a sixteen-year-old, Addy, whose best friend begins exhibiting signs of withdrawal and depression, it's a quick read. In the novella, it comes to light that a visiting uncle has been sexually abusing Addy's friend, and she didn't know what to do about it because of his threats. The book also has elements of teenage humor and involves a plot about time travel, kind of *Alice in Wonderland* meets Madeleine L'Engle. I suggest it as helpful to parents and teens as a discussion starter about family sexual abuse.

If you were raised in a Christian home where you were kept safe, you probably trust your family members. However, it is sad to say, such trust can be misplaced. We parents must provide supervision with our children even when they are with family members. You may think you know your family members well because you were raised in the same household as your siblings.

But you cannot assume that your experiences were the same as your siblings'—your siblings interacted with people outside the family you did not interact with. They had experiences you did not have.

In fact, given the secrecy that often surrounds sexual abuse, your siblings may have experienced sexual abuse as children that you don't know about. Since your siblings have left home, you have traveled different paths. The experiences your siblings have had since they left home will impact their parenting as well. In addition, their spouses impact their parenting style.

If your siblings have experienced sexual abuse, they may not be able to recognize the signs and symptoms of their own children acting as abusers or victims. Your siblings may not provide the same type of supervision and protection for their children as you provide for your children.

Unfortunately, the same is true of your spouse. I recently counseled in a case where a young mother discovered her husband molesting their children in the bathtub. Soon it came to light that the husband had himself been abused as a child—something of which his wife was completely unaware until the bathtub incident.

Research shows that sexual abuse is more likely to occur in families in which there are rigid gender roles, power imbalances, differential treatment of children in the family, and lack of parental supervision. (Rigid gender roles refers to the father being viewed as the person who has all the power in the family, with everyone else being submissive.[1])

Even parents who provide excellent parenting and supervision may have children who have been sexually abused. Unfortunately, an abused child can perpetuate abuse. Those children who have been sexually abused for long periods or repeatedly are more likely to abuse other children. However, the overwhelming majority of children who are abused never go on to abuse others.

Children who are exposed to sexual activity through abuse do not have the capacity to understand the boundaries of sexuality. For example, a mom I know who's particularly vigilant had a new foster child in the living room with her other children. As the mom turned to answer the phone, within the time it took her to walk across the room to replace the phone on a table, the new four-year-old had stripped her three-year-old's pants off.

If children who have been sexually abused begin to engage in sexual behavior with other children, they must be closely supervised by an adult. Young children do not have the intellectual ability or the impulse control to be able to manage overwhelming sexual thoughts and urges. These children need adults to provide boundaries and guidelines for them. A good rule of thumb is that children who are struggling with sexual impulses need "belt loop" supervision. This requires children to be close enough to an adult to grab hold of the adult's belt loop. Such children need this close supervision to learn how to interact appropriately and to help manage their sexual thoughts and impulses.

Disclosure of Abuse

How prevalent is delayed disclosure of this situation? Sometimes when children leave home for the military or for college, such secrets come to light as young people seek validation or support from their peers for what happened to them in childhood. I can't tell you how shocked I was when several of my college friends began telling me of family sexual abuse they'd undergone. I was naïve—such a thing never occurred to me because I'd grown up in a loving and vigilant family. But these young women were still hurting from what had happened to them.

Disclosure of sexual abuse between children in a family usually follows a pattern of (1) being known only to the children involved to (2) becoming known by other family members or members of the community. Rarely do children themselves disclose being abused by another child in the family. In the rare situations when children do disclose abuse by another child in the family, they generally tell their parents. Usually the abuse ends because the abuser grows up and leaves the family situation. But at any stage of the child's life, when abuse by another child in the family is discovered or disclosed, a family crisis often occurs. Loyalty to both children—the perpetrator and the victim—creates divided alliances in families.

The Bible tells a gut-wrenching story about sibling rape. One of King David's sons, Amnon, forced his younger stepsister into sexual relations even though she begged him not to do so (2 Samuel 13.) There's an important insight in this story: While Amnon had first said he "was in love" with Tamar, after he raped her, he "hated her with intense hatred" that was far stronger than any so-called love before. This is true in most cases—the perpetrator may profess affection for a child but ends up despising the vulnerable young person they abuse.

Remember: *Love protects. It does not violate.*

What Constitutes Sexual Abuse Between Children?

As parents, we see our children as nonsexual, but the reality is that all of us are sexual beings, even children. Children will explore their own and each other's bodies by looking and touching. Even at a young age, children get curious and may peek into the bathroom or try to watch when someone is changing clothes. As kids get older, they will use technology to find out more information about sex.

Once we acknowledge that children are sexual beings, it is important that as parents we learn to distinguish between what is common sexual behavior and sexual behaviors that are not common for children at different ages. There are some characteristics of sexual behavior that will help you evaluate whether the behavior is common or uncommon.

Typical Sexual Behaviors in Children

Sexual behaviors that are more typical in children will generally have the following traits:

- The sexual play is between children who typically play together.
- The sexual play is between children of similar size, age, and development.
- The sexual play is lighthearted. For example, the children may be giggling when they are discovered.
- When adults set limits, children follow the rules.

Characteristics of Sexual Abuse Between Children

In contrast, sexual *abuse* between children in a family involves a range of sexual behaviors in childhood that are not age-appropriate. Several criteria help distinguish between common sexual behavior and sexual abuse. These criteria include

- the age gap between the children;
- whether one child was coerced or tricked;
- the duration, frequency, and severity of the sexual activity; and
- whether the sexual activity was for the gratification of one child.

The chart on page 75 outlines common sexual behaviors and uncommon sexual behaviors based on children's ages.[2] Please note: My use of this chart doesn't condone all the behaviors that are "common"; for instance, a child losing his or her virginity at age thirteen to sixteen. But engaging in that behavior does not necessarily mark a child as a sexual offender or a victim of abuse. Knowing that such things are common in our culture, however, may alert you to extra protectiveness for your child.

Protecting Your Child in Your Family

Understanding common and uncommon sexual behaviors in children is the first step to protecting your child while interacting with family members. Here are some of the other steps you can take to protect your children:

1. *Don't let your guard down.* When we are with family members and friends, we tend to let our guard down and not provide the supervision we would provide if we were with strangers. We need to physically see our children to make sure they are safe. We can't turn that supervision over to other relatives.

2. *Talk to your children.* Let your children know that we love family members, but that even family members can make bad decisions. Your children need to know that no one can touch their private parts, not even a sibling or cousins.

3. *Explain how "games" may not be safe.* Other children, teens, and even adults may engage children in sexual abuse by disguising the abuse as a game. That's what happened to Amber. Your children need to know that they shouldn't play games that make them uncomfortable, that involve

Age	Common Behaviors	Uncommon Behaviors
0–5 Years	○ Questions about gender and private parts ○ Questions about hygiene and toileting ○ Questions about pregnancy and birth ○ Exploring genitals and experiencing pleasure ○ Showing and looking at private parts	○ Knowledge of specific sexual acts or use of explicit language ○ Engaging in adult-like sexual contact with other children
6–8 Years	○ Questions about physical development, relationships, sexual behavior ○ Questions about menstruation and pregnancy ○ Questions about personal values and sexuality ○ Experimenting with same-age and same-gender children during games or role-playing ○ Self-stimulation in private	○ Adult-like sexual behaviors ○ Knowledge of specific sexual acts ○ Behaving sexually in a public place or through technology
9–12 Years	○ Increased sexual awareness, feelings, and interest at the onset of puberty ○ Questions about sexual behavior and relationships ○ Discussing sexual acts and personal values ○ Increased experimentation with sexual behaviors ○ Self-stimulation in private	○ Regularly occurring adult-like sexual behavior ○ Behaving sexually in a public place or through technology
13–16 Years	○ Questions about social relationships and sexual customs ○ Questions about personal consequences and sexual behaviors ○ Self-stimulation in private ○ Sexual experimentation with individuals of the same age and gender is common. ○ Voyeuristic behaviors are common in this age group. ○ First sexual intercourse will occur for approximately one third of teens.	○ Behaving sexually in a public place or through technology ○ Masturbation in a public place ○ Sexual interest directed toward much younger children

touching their private parts or those of another person, or cause them to remove their clothes or the clothes of anyone else.

4. *Explain how wrestling and tickling can become unsafe.* Frequently perpetrators will engage children by tickling them or wrestling with them. Help your children understand that they can tell a family member to stop wrestling with them or to stop tickling them. Your children should not be alone with a family member who is insisting on these actions. If a family member wrestles with your children or tickles them when they are alone, your child should leave immediately. If your children cannot leave immediately, they should yell for help.

5. *Set clear family guidelines* for personal privacy and behavior. Discuss them with all members of your family and model respecting these guidelines.

- Children should not be expected to hug or kiss relatives they do not know.

- Emphasize the importance of respecting closed doors. Children should recognize that when they are changing clothes or using the restroom, the door should be closed; when a door is closed, children should knock before entering.

- Similarly, they should expect others to knock before opening their closed door.

- Children should also learn that when they have guests in their home, they need to play in the living room or other shared spaces in the home. As adults, we do not invite guests into our bedrooms. Similarly, we should teach children that their friends need to remain in shared spaces in the home rather than private spaces.

6. *Discuss these guidelines with any other adults* who spend time around or supervise the children. (If adults do not respect your family boundaries, reevaluate where and when you will spend time with them.)

7. *Let children know* that if they are not comfortable being around a particular adult or older child, then you or another adult will let that person know this (for instance, you will tell him that you don't want your child to sit on his lap).

8. As a child matures, *boundaries may need to change* (for example, you knock on the door before entering the room of an adolescent).

Final Thoughts

Perhaps in no other situation of sexual abuse can a parent so closely identify with God, the ultimate Parent. God as Father watches His children sinning against each other constantly, and it grieves His heart as it would any parent.

I urge anyone who suspects that a child has been abused by a sibling or other child who is a close relative to seek spiritual help. Such a situation will overwhelm you unless you have someone to stand by your side and point you to Scripture and methods of coping with the bitter choices that must be made.

Remember that child offenders may be acting out what was done to them. That doesn't excuse abuse, but it does give a parent a way to begin to understand and deal with the offender.

Messages for Your Child

Keep nurturing that warrior heart. Kids can learn to safeguard themselves if you give them the tools. Keep telling them these protective truths:

1. Children have the right to say no to anyone who asks them to do anything painful, embarrassing, or wrong.
2. No one can touch them on the parts of the body covered by a bathing suit, and they should not touch anyone else in these private places.
3. They must tell you immediately if someone tells them to keep a secret or tries to threaten them or bribe them. Assure them repeatedly that you will always be glad to know that, and they will not be in trouble.
4. If they find themselves alone with an adult or peer in an isolated area where others cannot see them or in an unfamiliar place, they need to leave the situation immediately.

If You Suspect Abuse

There are warning signs of abuse that your child may display, but *remember not all children who are being sexually abused will have these signs.* These red flags are when children

1. have physical injuries or have concerns about their genitalia;
2. display an unprecedented shyness about getting undressed in front of others;
3. express an unusual interest in sexual subjects or completely avoid sexual topics;

4. avoid individuals for no apparent reason or don't want to participate in certain activities;

5. experience sleep disturbances, bedwetting, or soiling; or

6. isolate themselves, are depressed, and have suicidal thoughts.

While these are all symptoms of sexual abuse, no single symptom will confirm a child has been sexually abused. If your child is exhibiting one or more of these symptoms, talk with him or her to make sure your child has not been abused.

If you suspect your child has been sexually or physically abused, remember not to overreact emotionally in front of your child. Let the child know you want to keep him or her safe—that it's your job, and you want to do it.

Take your concerns to a doctor, a social worker, or the police. You don't have to *know* that your child is not safe, you just have to suspect it to seek out professional assistance. And of course, don't leave your child in the same situation if you are concerned about his or her safety.

7

Abuse by Strangers

At the Restaurant

Meghan sits in my office, apparently unable to fill out the questionnaire on the clipboard I've handed her. Her minister called yesterday and asked if I could work Meghan and her five-year-old son, Josiah, into my schedule. The minister said Meghan seemed to be a great mom to Josiah—involved in church, happy attitude—and that Josiah was a well-behaved little boy. But the minister wanted my help because Meghan told him that her son had been sexually abused at a playground at a neighborhood fast-food restaurant.

"What happened is my fault," Meghan says, and her voice catches in her throat. Her short, streaked blond hair looks like she has rubbed it repeatedly and it stands up in what I think are unintentional tufts.

Meghan continues, "If I had been paying attention, this never would have happened. I had my head buried in my phone."

I sense that she needs to tell me some background to ease into the painful event. I ask her about what part of town she lives in. She describes an upscale neighborhood.

"It's a beautiful house, but after a while, I just feel cooped up in it," she says. "Like the walls are closing in on me. I love being a stay-at-home mom, but sometimes I feel all alone. I used to work before we had Josiah. I miss being around people at work."

I nod and listen.

"It's worse in the winter. When it's cold, I can't let Josiah play outside. He's all boy," she smiles, "and if he doesn't get some time outside, he is impossible all day long. So after breakfast in the morning, those days when it's cold or windy, I take Josiah to play at the fast-food restaurant because it has a big indoor playground that he loves. While he plays, I get some time to relax and catch up with my friends on my phone.

"I think of myself as a good mom." She looks up at me, almost defiantly, but immediately drops her eyes. "I thought it was safe for Josiah at the playground. There were just other kids on the playground. I mean, there were a few regular moms that we see almost every day sitting and chatting, but they weren't anywhere near Josiah. Sometimes I would talk with a couple of the moms, but I spent most of my time shopping online or texting my friends or looking at their posts online. It was so nice to just interact with adults for a few minutes, even if it was in cyberspace. Was that so wrong?"

"Of course moms need time for themselves and interaction with other adults," I reassure her. "But something changed?"

She nods and composes herself. "A week or so ago, Josiah started whining and crying every time we would pull up to the restaurant. He'd say he didn't feel good or that he wanted to play at home. Then last Thursday he threw a huge tantrum, and I gave up and took him back home. After he settled down, I asked him why he didn't want to go to the playground. At first he said he didn't like playing with Lamar—that's another one of the kids there. He wouldn't tell me why, so I kept asking him. . . ." Her voice trails off.

I tell Meghan that we will help Josiah deal with whatever had happened to him.

"Josiah told me that Lamar hurt his bottom. At first I thought he meant Lamar was slapping his bottom, but Josiah said that Lamar pulled his pants down and hurt the inside of his bottom. . . . Then I knew what he was saying."

She looks me in the eye again. "And you know what the worst part is? When he was playing, I heard him yell a couple times, but when he quieted down I thought it was just because he was mad at another kid for pushing him or something. Now I realize he was in trouble and I didn't do anything."

"But you *did* do something, once you knew."

Meghan tells me she immediately called Child Protective Services to report what happened, and I nod confirmation that she did a good thing. Child Protective Services sent Josiah for a physical exam and then for an interview at the Child Advocacy Center. The exam showed that Josiah had been anally penetrated.

Meghan is overcome with grief and regret and second-guessing of herself. "How could I have let that happen to him?" she says. "I was right there at the playground and didn't know what was going on. What kind of a mother am I?"

"Even with excellent supervision, sexual abuse can happen," I tell her. "But our focus now has to be on how to help Josiah cope with what has already happened. Beating yourself up because of what is past is not a good use of your energy. Josiah needs you in the here and now, interacting with him. We can get through this!"

One of the reasons I can confidently assure her is that in this kind of incident, a child might not interpret what happened as a sexual incident. All he knows is that someone hurt him. Because of that, it would be much like recovering from physical abuse.

Incidents like this one can occur in playgrounds and play areas anywhere. What follows applies to all play situations.

The Role of Distraction

With technology literally at our fingertips, it is easier than ever for parents to be distracted. An entire online world of apps and games can grab our attention in seconds and pull us in for much longer than we realize because people lose track of time when using technology.

With our eyes on a screen, we stop paying attention to what is going on around us, and when we do look up, there's a lag time as our consciousness switches gears. Jesus said that you can't serve two masters, and never is this truer than when you're mentally engaged online and thinking you can properly supervise your children. If you can't hear what's going on around you and don't glance up from your device regularly and mindfully, then stow that device when you are supervising your children. If you want to immerse yourself in technology, then another adult should be supervising your children—without distractions—while you are using technology.

It's not just technology—we can get so involved in conversations that we don't pay attention to what is going on around us. If you tend to get immersed in conversations, set an alarm on your phone to remind you to stop and check on your children. Don't lose track of time or your children.

Be aware not only of time, but of distances. Your children should be within eyesight at all times and close enough for you to hear them. If you're deep in conversation or on your device, by the time you look up, they can be a hundred yards away from you and can barely hear you call to them.

Survey the Surroundings

When you first get to a playground, take time to walk around it. Look for places where your child would be concealed from you, where another person—child or adult—could interact with your child without your knowledge. There are blind spots in any location. Once you locate the blind spots on a playground such as hedges or walls, know that you will have to get up and move as needed to provide appropriate supervision of your children.

Many playgrounds are built with lots of enclosed spaces, especially those with tunnels, passageways, and "corral" areas with balls or other objects. It is difficult to supervise your children in playgrounds with lots of enclosed spaces. Every enclosed space holds the potential for your child to be hurt.

Don't Let Your Guard Down

When you go to the same playground or play area, its familiarity can make you less alert. Remember that your child can be safe for days at a time, but that doesn't mean that the same location will be safe all the time. And it's not just adults you must watch: Children may be experiencing abuse and not realize it is not appropriate to interact sexually with other kids.

One of the easiest places to let your guard down is at play areas at church. On many occasions I've gone to church and seen children playing without any supervision at all. I think how easy it would be for someone to abuse those children. We need to recognize that not everyone around us sees the world the way we do.

Tag Out

Like Meghan, we all need breaks from parenting. Face it: Supervising children is emotionally and mentally draining, and no one can be on the top of her game all the time. Rather than taking your children to a playground so you have a break from parenting, get another trusted, vetted adult to watch your children when you need a break. If you can't afford to hire someone, trade off on the supervision with your spouse or with other mothers. You *do* need a break, and you *do* need time to take care of yourself—just plan well for those breaks. Schedule them at regular intervals *before* you are completely worn out.

Pay Attention

Imagine each time you are around a play area that you will be called upon to give a physical description of each person there. While the situation here is a child offending against a child, an adult can abuse a child in a play area just as easily. A sexual assault can take place in mere seconds—a sudden action that nonetheless will be the end stage of careful planning on the part of an adult offender. For a predator, a park or playground offers the opportunity to scout out and fantasize: a playground for the pedophile imagination. Any adult who intently looks at your child or who tries to engage your child in play or conversation could pose a threat to your child.

Be Proactive

If someone tries to interact with your children or looks at them with frequency, just remove your children from the situation. Don't confront another adult. If you confront them, you may create an unsafe situation for yourself and your children. Take your children, get in the car, leave, and make sure you aren't followed. If anyone follows you, drive to the nearest police station.

Photographing Kids

With phone technology, it is difficult to monitor who is taking pictures of your children. While this discussion about photographing your kids could have been included in any section of the book, it is more likely that your young children will be photographed during play events or other activities with children. Be on the alert for people photographing your children.

In addition, carefully consider the risks you take when you post pictures of your children online. People can take pictures from your social media and digitally alter them so that they become sexually explicit. Be especially cautious about posting pictures with your children in bathtubs or partially clothed: What may look innocent and sweet to you can be manipulated by others to become sexually explicit. Watermark your photos so it is harder for others to manipulate them. Ask your friends and family to also be cautious about posting pictures of your children online. Once an image is online, it is available to strangers and could potentially be edited to be pornographic.

Bathroom Dangers

Once children are old enough to go to the bathroom independently, you need a strategy about how to negotiate public bathrooms. Individuals who are interested in sexually assaulting children will target bathrooms.

The ideal situation is to take your children only to restaurants and other businesses that have family restrooms, but that may not be an option. With children five and under, my recommendation is to always take them to the restroom with you even if they are not the same gender as you. Children under five do not have the capacity to protect themselves in a bathroom with strangers. Even when your children are a little bit older, make sure there are no other people in the restroom when you send your children in; if there are other people in the restroom, stand right outside and talk to your children as they go in, to let everyone in the bathroom hear you say that you are watching who comes in and out of the bathroom. While monitoring your children going to the bathroom can be a little hassle, it is worth the extra effort to keep your kids safe.

This situation is more difficult for single fathers than mothers, because taking your young daughter into a men's room with multiple stalls (with a urinal in the open, for instance) may not be a good idea. Asking an unknown woman to take your daughter into a women's bathroom isn't an option either. Perhaps the best strategy is to plan ahead and choose places with family restrooms. If not, be prepared to leave and go to a gas station or other place where you can protect your daughter in a single-stall bathroom.

Talk to Your Kids

1. Make sure your kids understand that it is never okay to play a game in which they get hurt physically. Just because something is a "game" doesn't mean it's fun, and it doesn't mean it's safe.

2. Help your children recognize that they don't have to participate in games just because someone invites them to participate—they have the right to say no to other people about any play activity they don't like or that doesn't feel safe. If you don't know how to start this kind of

87

conversation, think back to a time when your child was in a play situation he or she didn't like. Role-play with your child how to avoid the situation so that he or she is comfortable saying no to any game.

3. It's not okay to take off your clothes. By age four, children should understand that they need to keep their clothes on when they are not in their own bedroom or a bathroom, even if other kids are disrobing. If you find your children taking off their clothes, you need to redirect the behavior as you would any other undesirable behavior. Don't become overly emotional. Assume your child doesn't know the boundary or is ignoring the boundary and redirect the behavior.

4. With child safety, the "buddy system" doesn't always work. We shouldn't rely on the judgment of another child. Additionally, we need to equip our children to protect themselves because the buddy they are paired with may not be safe around them. Again, emphasize that it is good to come to us right away and tell us when something or someone is not safe.

5. Create, discuss, and enforce boundaries about where to play. When you arrive at a playground or play area, give your children specific physical boundaries about where they can and cannot play. For example: "You can't go past this blue bench," or, "If you can't see Mom's eyes, you are not in a safe place." If your child leaves the approved area, be consistent about enforcing the boundaries. It's far better to put up with their wails of protest as you take them home, and action is always better than an empty threat. This is how your children learn that you are serious about their safety—when they see that you're willing to inconvenience yourself for it.

Being watchful is a characteristic that is highly valued in the Bible, as it is mentioned more than fifty times. One of the passages where Jesus urged watchfulness is Mark 13. Although Jesus was talking about His own Second Coming, His words can apply to our need to not be distracted or lose focus on our tasks at hand:

> Keep watch! Stay awake! You do not know when that time will come. It's like a man going away. He leaves his house and puts his servants in charge. Each one is given a task to do. He tells the one at the door to keep watch.
>
> So keep watch! You do not know when the owner of the house will come back. It may be in the evening or at midnight. It may be when the rooster crows or at dawn. He may come suddenly. So do not let him find you sleeping. What I say to you, I say to everyone. "Watch!"
>
> Mark 13:33–37 NIrV

Messages for Your Child

Keep nurturing that warrior heart. Kids can learn to safeguard themselves if you give them the tools. Keep telling them these protective truths:

1. Children have the right to say no to anyone who asks them to do anything painful, embarrassing, or wrong.
2. No one can touch them on the parts of the body covered by a bathing suit, and they should not touch anyone else in these private places.
3. They must tell you immediately if someone tells them to keep a secret or tries to threaten them or bribe them.

Assure them repeatedly that you will always be glad to know that, and they will not be in trouble.

4. If they find themselves alone with an adult or peer in an isolated area where others cannot see them or in an unfamiliar place, they need to leave the situation immediately.

If You Suspect Abuse

There are warning signs of abuse that your child may display, but *remember not all children who are being sexually abused will have these signs.* These red flags are when children

1. have physical injuries or have concerns about their genitalia;
2. display an unprecedented shyness about getting undressed in front of others;
3. express an unusual interest in sexual subjects or completely avoid sexual topics;
4. avoid individuals for no apparent reason or don't want to participate in certain activities;
5. experience sleep disturbances, bedwetting, or soiling; or
6. isolate themselves, are depressed, and have suicidal thoughts.

While these are all symptoms of sexual abuse, no single symptom will confirm a child has been sexually abused. If your child is exhibiting one or more of these symptoms, talk with him or her to make sure your child has not been abused.

If you suspect your child has been sexually or physically abused, remember not to overreact emotionally in front of your child. Let the child know you want to keep him or her safe—that it's your job, and you want to do it.

Take your concerns to a doctor, a social worker, or the police. You don't have to *know* that your child is not safe, you just have to suspect it to seek out professional assistance. And of course, don't leave your child in the same situation if you are concerned about his or her safety.

Children Ages Six to Eleven

8

Children Six to Eleven

What They Should Know

Once your children become school age, their world expands and so should your vigilance. Here are some things you can expect of them and of yourself.

1. They will begin to take an active role in managing their own health and safety. They should know how to brush their teeth, bathe, and dress themselves. They should feel responsible for taking care of their own body.

2. Your children cannot tell you where they hurt if they do not know the vocabulary for all their body parts. I recently spoke with an ER nurse who said one of the biggest challenges in assessing young abuse victims (as well as even adult patients without sexual abuse who have urinary tract infections or other conditions) is that they don't know terms to identify their body parts.

3. Your children should know the correct terms for the body parts of the opposite sex as well. Knowing the correct terms for body parts will make it easier to communicate information to your children about sexuality as they grow up.

4. During the elementary school years, your children should develop an understanding that human sexuality is a natural part of life. When families lived on farms, there were natural opportunities for children to learn about reproduction and see it as a normal part of life. Today, we have to use other opportunities to communicate about sexuality. When you are pregnant or a friend or family member is pregnant, it provides an opportunity to teach your children that sex is a natural part of life and reproduction.

5. Perhaps one of the most difficult concepts for us to accept, much less teach, is that sexuality occurs across the human life-span. While many of us might like to believe that our parents had four children and therefore had sex only four times, the reality is generally very different. In a loving marriage, sexual encounters occur well into old age. Our children also need to be aware of this for safety reasons: When we recognize that sexual interest extends into old age, parents and children recognize that older individuals can pose a threat to our children.

6. During this stage of childhood, it is important that children be taught that sexual feelings are legitimate and normal. God created us to be sexual beings, and we all have sexual feelings. Having sexual feelings isn't bad or dirty. In fact, God made it so that the human race can't continue without sex! In the context of marriage, sexual feelings are beautiful. We don't want to inadvertently teach our

children that sexual feelings are bad. God created us with sexual feelings, and He said it is good.

7. Our tendency as parents is to wait until puberty hits to talk to our children about how puberty will impact their bodies. But by age ten, our children should already understand how their bodies will change during puberty. Puberty is occurring at earlier ages than before. On average, girls enter puberty at eleven years of age, while boys enter puberty at twelve. Nonetheless, there is great diversity in when puberty occurs in males and females. They will need general information about menstruation and wet dreams. Our children also need to understand that the onset of puberty will increase the occurrence of sexual feelings, which is normal.

8. As children prepare to enter puberty, they also need to understand how sexual acts can lead to reproduction, but that not every sexual act will result in pregnancy. (We know that, but a child may not. You should make that clear.) They need to understand how pregnancy occurs and ways to prevent pregnancy and STDs. Many parents believe that sharing this information with their children is giving permission to have sex. Actually, research and my experience show that being open in sharing this information *delays* sexual activity and helps your children recognize when they are in dangerous situations.

9. One of the best tools for sexual safety is having good relationship skills. Children who are able to develop and maintain healthy friendships are not as easily manipulated by predators. They are more secure in their ability to say no to activities they don't like or that are dangerous. Spending time helping your child develop good

relationships and learning how to resolve conflicts with peers is time well invested. When your children can negotiate difficult conversations about conflict in a friendship, they are better equipped to handle confrontations with peers or adults about inappropriate sexual overtures.

10. A particularly difficult skill to teach children regarding friendship is the difference between online friends and real friends. During the elementary years, your children will begin to have increased access to technology. A person can lie face-to-face, or they can lie online, and children aren't able to determine if a person is deceptive. For example, someone can say she is eight years old and post a picture of an eight-year-old but not actually *be* an eight-year-old.

11. Children need to learn to verify, not trust, people trying to be a "friend" in the virtual world. Ideally, children's contacts in the virtual world should be limited to friends they know in the real world.

12. Discuss safe and unsafe interactions on the Internet. For instance, they should never give out personal information to individuals or in apps. This includes information about their school or church, the city they live in, and any photos of the outside of their homes or buildings that could be identifiable (such as street signs, house numbers, or distinctive exterior features).

13. Similarly, they need to learn to report to parents any time a person or an app asks for a picture of them. An emoji or animal or fantasy character is always better as his or her profile picture than a real photograph of the child. Also, make sure your child doesn't choose images or names that include the word *baby* or other trigger words that attract pedophile attention.

14. Your job is to monitor your child's interaction with technology—which you certainly must do, lovingly, firmly, consistently. Countless online resources will help you set boundaries. One absolute rule should be that your child never have any electronic device that provides Internet access in his or her bedroom. Children are being exposed through multiple types of technology to sexual information. Don't enable that.

Even with excellent monitoring of your children's technology use, they will probably encounter inappropriate content. Expect that. Use those situations to teach your children.

A warrior heart is a realistic heart. It knows that we live in a dirty world. It acknowledges that the challenges of life are made harder by those who try deliberately to hurt children.

But a warrior heart is determined not to be caught up in anybody's schemes.

Jesus said to His disciples, "Things that cause people to stumble are bound to come, but woe to anyone through whom they come. It would be better for them to be thrown into the sea with a millstone tied around their neck than to cause one of these little ones to stumble. *So watch yourselves*" (Luke 17:1–3, italics added).

9

Abuse by Authority Figure

Private Lessons

A woman in my church, Teresa, called me with an unusual request.

"Our son Ethan is being asked to testify as a character witness in court next week, and I wonder if you could see him in your office and give him some pointers so he won't be so nervous?"

I scrolled through my memory and had a mental image of the family and their handsome teenage boy, Ethan.

"Did Ethan volunteer to do this, but now he's getting cold feet?"

I heard her hesitation.

"Not exactly. Well, at first he said he'd do it, but I guess it was my idea to begin with. I mean, we've known his guitar teacher, Richard, for years, for goodness' sake. He's like part of our family. We know so many other families that have had lessons with Richard. And now some kid is accusing Richard of 'sexually inappropriate behavior,' whatever that means, and we know it's a lie."

"When is Ethan supposed to testify?"

"Monday. I know that's only three days away, but I thought since you do this all the time, the expert witness thing . . ."

Now, the next day, Ethan sits before me in my office. He is a wiry sixteen-year-old who fidgets in his seat and taps one fingernail on the arm of his chair. His mom had dropped him off here, but he keeps glancing toward the door. He answers my opening questions about where he goes to school and what he's thinking about college, but his answers are polite and minimal.

"So this seems stressful for you, Ethan," I say. "What's bothering you?"

"I'm going to have to tell the truth in court."

"What is the truth?"

He looks away, and his mouth begins several words with no sound. We sit in silence for several minutes. Then he shrugs.

"The kid in court is telling the truth," he said. "Richard abused him."

"How do you know the other kid is telling the truth?"

"Because Richard abused *me*."

I listen as Ethan describes how Richard had been his guitar teacher since he was nine. At one point, Richard told Ethan's parents that their son had extraordinary talents and that he was willing to provide extra instruction to help him develop his "gift."

"Mom was thrilled, and she would drop me off for the last lesson of the day and she'd go run errands. At first, it was all fine. We'd have the lesson and then I'd just watch videos until Mom came back. But then one day, like out of the blue, it was a porn video. And then a different porn video after every lesson."

I nod. "But it wasn't just porn, with Richard?"

Ethan looks down.

"No, one day he asks me to take my clothes off so he could take some pictures of me. I said, 'No way!' but then he said he'd tell my mom I'd sneaked in some porn to play on his DVD player and he didn't know where I got it."

Haltingly, Ethan tells me of situations that progressed from videos of him naked—coerced with the threat of telling his parents—to ongoing sexual assault that Richard videotaped.

I choose my words carefully. "Is this still going on?"

For the first time, Ethan seems to relax a little bit, but his words are bitter.

"Once my voice started changing and . . ." he rubs his chin and upper lip, "Richard seemed to kinda lose interest, and the extra guitar lessons slowed down. I finally was able to quit the lessons."

I knew the pattern. The pedophile had moved on to another preadolescent boy.

"But my folks stayed friends with him, and when he was at our house, he acted like nothing had ever happened. Sometimes I wondered if I had just imagined the whole thing. But then Richard started complaining to my parents that some kids were trying to cause trouble for him, when he had been completely blameless. Richard said he was the victim, and then my parents volunteered me to be a character witness."

Rarely am I stunned by a situation, but this one did it. Ethan's anxiety wasn't just about talking in front of an audience. He couldn't bear the thought of his parents learning the truth when he testified. Ethan was taking the oath to tell the truth dead seriously. He never considered *not* telling the truth in court, not for one moment.

I sat in deep respect for someone so young with such a deep sense of morality.

We discussed ways we could handle the situation other than letting his parents learn in court of the abuse he'd suffered. I offered to help him tell his parents in my office. When his parents arrived, Ethan told them that he had been sexually abused by Richard and that he was going to tell the truth in court on Monday.

Of course, his parents were stunned, and then they went through a range of natural emotions. But toward their son, Ethan's parents were reassuring and nurturing as they helped him understand that they were not angry with him and that they loved him.

Ultimately, we called the lead detective on the case, and he met with Ethan and his family. With Ethan's additional information, Richard was persuaded to take a plea deal that put him in prison, and Ethan was spared having to testify in court. And with counseling and time, Ethan is putting the situation behind him.

Do Your Homework

Before your child begins to engage in private lessons, dance, gymnastics, or club sports teams, you need to check out the reputation of the institution or the individual involved. You should conduct a background search much like you would if you were hiring a nanny. The instructors or coaches who interact with your children will have access and opportunity to sexually abuse your children.

Here are some strategies:

1. Ask the instructor for names of other children he or she has taught and the contact information for their parents. Call the parents and ask if they have any concerns about the instructor. Did their children enjoy the activity, or express dread or other negative feelings?

2. Find out if the instructor provides one-on-one instruction or extra instruction that favors certain children or has special provisions for some children. Though not a certain sign of a pedophile, this is a red flag.

3. Use search engines such as Google and social media to check the reputation of the individual or organizations

you are considering giving access to your children. You can learn a lot about individuals and organizations through Facebook and other Internet sources. If other parents are not happy with the instructor or organization, read what they have to say. One or two disgruntled individuals can be expected, but pay close attention if a pattern emerges of several parents having concerns, particularly if it appears across more than one time period. If this research leaves you with any concerns about an organization or instructor, find a different option for your child.

4. If you feel good about the instructor or organization after doing a background check, ask to attend some instruction sessions or practices. Be sure that you like the way the instructor or coach interacts with other children.

5. Once your child starts taking lessons or participating in practices, attend the practices or sessions regularly. If you can't attend all the lessons or practices, drop by at irregular and unexpected times to make sure the situation is safe.

6. In some cases, you may want to provide electronic supervision through a phone or nanny cam. Any instructor or coach who is being appropriate should not be resistant to you wanting to know what is going on in lessons or a practice.

Questions to Ask Your Kids

The first step in keeping your kids safe is open communication. Parents do lots of talking to our kids, but we also need to learn the right questions to ask. Often we ask a generic question like "How was your practice?" or "How was your lesson?" More specific questions will give you valuable insight. Some of the questions we can ask include:

- What would you change about practice?
- What made you feel happy in practice?
- What made you feel sad in practice?
- Did you learn something you'd never known before?
- Did something surprise you today?
- Did you do anything different today?
- Did you feel comfortable in practice today?
- Did your teacher give you any compliments?
- Did you feel worried at any time during practice?
- Did you feel scared at any time during practice?

Of course, you wouldn't ask all these questions at once. But by asking specific questions, you will get more specific information from your children, and you will be much more likely to notice if something changes in your child's world.

"How Could a Friend Act Like Nothing Happened?"

Ethan's situation with his guitar teacher was made much worse because his parents became closer friends with his abuser, while Ethan began to doubt his own grasp on the reality of the situation because Richard acted so "normal" around him and his family.

We all tend to believe that other people are like us, and that they will naturally feel guilt in situations where we would feel guilt. We expect other people to have the same sense of betrayal that we have. The reality is that each person is unique. Just because you or I might feel guilt does not mean another person will.

It's difficult to wrap our minds around the idea that a friend could sexually abuse one of our children and then continue to interact with us as though nothing happened. However, individuals who would sexually abuse our children do not think the same way we do. They often convince themselves that our children are seducing them or that our children are in love with them. They might actually blame our children for the sexual abuse or blame us for not supervising their relationship closely enough.

Face it: Most of us are not naturally adept at recognizing who might sexually abuse our children. We have preconceived ideas that blind us about who would hurt our children. It's difficult to visualize any friend doing that.

The Biggest Warning Sign

The biggest warning sign that adults might have a sexual interest in your children is that they will seek out time alone with your children.

But before they do that, they will strategize and lay groundwork. The foundation upon which they will build a structure of abuse is *your* trust of them. They will be charming and likeable and may even seem sacrificial and serving. They will seem to affirm your justifiable pride in your children and your need to have your children succeed. They may sympathize with your rushed lifestyle.

They may use flattery or favorable comparisons to their other students. They may refer back to years of their experience in judging when a child has "potential" or extraordinary talent. They may point to success stories of kids they have helped achieve in a sport or skill.

Then you will gladly grant them time alone with your children.

Watching out for a predator in your child's life? It's most likely not the skulking stranger. It is the adult you've come to trust, who will manage to get one-on-one time with your children.

In today's world, a responsible private instructor or coach knows that spending one-on-one time repeatedly with the same children will raise red flags. Responsible instructors or coaches with healthy boundaries will work hard to assure that they don't repeatedly spend one-to-one time with children because they don't want to be accused of inappropriate behavior. They will avoid even the "appearance of evil" (1 Thessalonians 5:22 KJV).

Two Wrongs Don't Make a Right

I remember my mom saying that two wrongs don't make a right. (She was usually saying this because one of the four kids in our family wanted to retaliate against a sibling who they believed had committed an offense against him or her. Frontier justice, kid-style.)

However, this concept of "two wrongs don't make a right" is very important to convey to your children with another very practical application: Children need to know that if they have done something wrong, doing something else wrong to cover it up will just make things worse. That's how Richard was able to graduate Ethan from watching a pornographic video (which Ethan knew his parents would disapprove of) to actual participation in sexual acts. Richard created a "need" in Ethan to cover up the video watching, which allowed Richard to move on to the next stage of abuse.

Though his parents were good people, they never made it plain to Ethan that if he did something wrong and someone was trying to blackmail or coerce him because of this, he should tell them and they would listen.

How can you avoid such a situation? Tell your kids that you will always work with them, not against them, if they do something wrong. There may be consequences, but there will also be love, forgiveness, and growth forward.

Role-play situations with your child regarding encounters with pornography or other online temptations. Let them know they can come to you immediately if someone tries to coerce them. Tell them that this is a train that can either run downhill without brakes or you can keep it in the station.

A very powerful Bible passage is one I recommend that you memorize with your children: "For the grace of God has appeared that offers salvation to all people. *It teaches us to say 'No' to ungodliness and worldly passions,* and to live self-controlled, upright and godly lives in this present age" (Titus 2:11–12, italics added).

The first part of this passage says that only grace, God's gift to us, saves us. Human effort alone can't do that. But we're not on our own fighting evil. That gift of God teaches us to have warrior hearts. Specifically, we can say "NO!" and do it loudly and with confidence when evil gets right up in our face.

Post this verse on your refrigerator or other places everyone in your family can see it. Explain it. Memorize it with your kids and practice it, shouting the word *NO!* as you say it. Make up and act out scenarios in which you as an adult would have to say NO! to keeping a wallet you find on the sidewalk; NO! to a suggestion you drink alcohol before driving; NO! to someone who would make fun of a disabled or vulnerable person. Then role-play with your children similar situations they might face with money, substances, pornography, and inappropriate touching.

Our primary job is to keep our kids safe. Ethan's story highlights the issue of porn. You should have conversations about porn with your children while they are in early elementary school. I became aware of this kind of problem when one of the children living in my home several years ago struggled to tell me that all the boys in his third-grade class were passing around porn. (This happened so long ago that kids were still looking at pictures rather than videos.) He didn't want to look at the pictures, but the other kids made fun of him for not looking, and he wanted to fit in. He began to have behavioral issues at school because he felt guilty for looking at the pornography, but didn't want to tell any adults and be a "tattletale."

Now, if this was an issue years ago, before kids carried cell phones to school, it is so much worse today with cell phones and Internet access. Our children need to know that it is okay to tell us if their peers or other adults are showing them porn. Let them know that it is our job to keep them safe and that watching porn is not safe.

Also—and this is vitally important—we must be trustworthy if our children tell us that other people are showing them porn. Being trustworthy means we don't set our children up to be bullied by peers because they told someone. There are ways to handle situations where porn is being shown by peers without throwing our children under the bus. For instance, we can contact authorities in a school or other organization and request that they check on what kids are viewing on their phones or on computers. We can express concern without identifying our child as the one who told us about the situation.

Messages for Your Child

Keep nurturing that warrior heart. Kids can learn to safeguard themselves if you give them the tools. Keep telling them these protective truths:

1. Children have the right to say no to anyone who asks them to do anything painful, embarrassing, or wrong.

2. No one can touch them on the parts of the body covered by a bathing suit, and they should not touch anyone else in these private places.

3. They must tell you immediately if someone tells them to keep a secret or tries to threaten them or bribe them. Assure them repeatedly that you will always be glad to know that, and they will not be in trouble.

4. Children have the right to refuse to look at pictures or videos of other people who are naked or engaged in sexual activities.

5. If they find themselves alone with an adult or peer in an isolated area where others cannot see them or in an unfamiliar place, they need to leave the situation immediately.

6. Children need to be aware of peers or adults who make jokes about or talk about sexual information. Your children need to know that God created sex to form a special bond between men and women who are married. They need to tell you if peers or adults are joking about sexual content or talking about sexual information with them.

7. Children need to know that talking about sexual information with friends or viewing sexual content does not make them more grown up. Rather, talking about sexual information or viewing pornographic information will likely confuse them about God's plan for sex.

If You Suspect Abuse

There are warning signs of abuse that your child may display, but *remember not all children who are being sexually abused will show these signs*. These red flags are when children

1. exhibit behaviors that change drastically or they are emotional;
2. express an unusual interest in sexual subjects or completely avoid sexual topics;
3. avoid individuals for no apparent reason or don't want to participate in certain activities;
4. experience sleep disturbances, bedwetting, or soiling; or
5. isolate themselves, are depressed, and have suicidal thoughts.

While these are all symptoms of sexual abuse, no single symptom will confirm a child has been sexually abused. If your child is exhibiting one or more of these symptoms, talk with him or her to make sure he or she has not been abused.

If you suspect your child has been sexually or physically abused, remember not to overreact emotionally in front of your child. Let the child know you want to keep him or her safe—that it's your job, and you want to do it.

Take your concerns to a doctor, a social worker, or the police. You don't have to know that your child is not safe, you just have to suspect it to seek out professional assistance. And of course, don't leave your child in the same situation if you are concerned about their safety.

10

Abuse by Family/Trusted Friends

The Sleepover

Emily, a woman with short brown hair and reddened eyes, scrapes the chair away from the table and sits down. She folds her arms and leans across the table toward me.

"Glad to meet you, Dr. Robinson," she says, "but I want you to know—*we* want you to know—that we are here pretty much against our will. In fact, this feels like a witch hunt." Her voice ends on a sob.

Her husband, Caleb, his baseball cap pushed back on his head, sits down too, and nods in agreement. "This is just stupid." He takes off his cap and turns it around in his hands before laying it on the table. "No offense meant to you," he tells me, his voice softening, and puts his arm around his wife.

"None taken." I look down at the transcript of the forensic (legal) interview their daughter Samantha had taken part in three days before. Although I know what Samantha said in the interview, I need to reassure her parents and help them get through this experience. But first I have to help them accept that something bad truly had occurred.

"You've had a hard couple of days," I say. "Bring me up to speed on what's happened."

As I listen, I can see that their anger comes out of their confusion and fear. Caleb's and Emily's world shattered with a phone call from an investigator at the district attorney's office three days earlier. The investigator told Emily that another child who attended a sleepover had told her mother that a man had touched her inappropriately at the sleepover.

Their daughter Samantha had been at that same sleepover. The investigator asked Emily and Caleb to bring Samantha to the Child Advocacy Center for an interview. Stunned, Emily called Caleb at work and asked him what he thought. No way, he said. They were good friends with the parents, Jim and Tina, who hosted the sleepover. Nothing could have happened.

They didn't want to subject their innocent eight-year-old, Samantha, to a stranger asking a lot of questions about sex, just because another kid had told a story. Only when the investigator told them that he could get a court order for Samantha's interview did they reluctantly agree.

The investigator tried to address some of their fears by explaining that the interview would take place at the Child Advocacy Center, where a trained forensic interviewer and child-friendly, age-appropriate interview rooms would make the experience as easy on Samantha as possible. In addition, the interview would be recorded so that Samantha—like any child who may have been abused—wouldn't have to be interviewed multiple times.

"But they told us not to ask Samantha any questions first," Emily says. "We could have cleared this all up in minutes, but they said it could impact the interview, so we tried to carry on like everything was normal for two more days, like we go to the

Child Advocacy Center every day." She laughs, a bitter, tearful laugh.

"And then when we get to the investigator's office, they tell us again we can't go in the room with her, can't even watch it." Caleb picks up the hat and begins rubbing the brim, back and forth, back and forth, the motions of a protector who isn't allowed to protect.

"It's so stupid," he says. "We go on camping trips with Jim and Tina, have for years," he says. "I'd trust them with my life. There is no way that Jim would have touched Samantha or any other little girl at that party."

Emily nods vigorously, and they both look in my eyes for validation.

"We need to talk about what Samantha told the investigator in the interview," I say. Both parents literally hold their breath. They cast a glance toward the nearby room where Samantha is playing a board game with one of my interns.

"Let me explain how the interview was conducted, and what I know from the report." I pat the papers on my desk, just a light tap to show them that I have a record of it. "The interviewer was very gentle with Samantha. He started by asking her about her school and her friends. Then he asked her to tell him if she knew the difference between the truth and a lie."

Emily and Caleb nod again.

"Of course, Samantha did great—you've done a good job with her. She knew what's a true thing and what's a lie. Then the investigator asked her about the sleepover—which of her friends were there, what they ate, what games they played."

"And she told them just what she told us," Caleb interrupts. "We saw all the girls when we dropped her off. And they ate pizza and watched a Disney movie and ate popcorn, and went to bed all in the same room in their sleeping bags, and we picked her up the next morning."

"And she was *fine*," Emily says, half rising from her chair. "So just let us take her home."

But what Samantha told them was only part of the truth.

The night of the party, by the time the movie was over, some of the girls were sleepy and wanted to go to bed. Samantha and two of the other girls started to watch another movie, but fell asleep only a few minutes into the movie.

Sometime during the night, Samantha got up to go to the bathroom. The lights in the hall had been left on so the girls could find the bathroom, so Samantha had no trouble finding her way. When she came out of the bathroom and started down the hall, she felt a strong hand wrap around her mouth. A man whispered to her, telling her to do exactly what he said, or else he would hurt her parents.

The man pulled Samantha into a bedroom and had her get down on her knees and perform oral sex on him. When he was finished, he shoved Samantha back into the hall and repeated that he would kill her parents.

Samantha stumbled down the hall and went back to her sleeping bag. She lay awake for most of the rest of the night, too scared to go back to sleep.

"But now she's glad she could tell someone," I say to the parents.

Caleb is on his feet, his face red with rage. "Jim? My friend Jim?!"

"No," I say. "It was his brother who was spending the night with them, on his way to California."

The next minutes are again tense and tearful and furious and horrific—and unfortunately, a scene I have witnessed many times when parents face the unthinkable.

Then comes the guilt. Caleb and Emily allowed their daughter to stay at a friend's home where this happened. They feel like they had been naïve to trust their friends with supervising their daughter. They have nothing in their parenting skills of the past to use in this situation. How will they talk to Samantha; how will they help her? Who can help them?

As devastating as this is, there are people and resources for families facing such situations. Within the next weeks, I will begin counseling with both parents and child to help them put the pieces of their lives back together. I know they're motivated; I know they can do this.

Why Sleepovers Are Risky

Sleepovers place children in a vulnerable situation: They find themselves alone and in a bed outside the care of their parents. Though surrounded by peers, there is typically only minimal adult supervision.

I didn't want to allow the children in my home to feel this particular kind of vulnerability early in their lives, thus they have stayed at their grandparents' homes and with aunts and uncles, but they have not stayed at friends' homes.

As you decide whether your children will attend sleepovers, it is important that you consider some research.

- First, most children are sexually abused in a place familiar to them. This means your own home, a relative's home, or a friend's home. Furthermore, the location of an incident of sexual abuse is likely to be at a place your child has been before.
- Second, sexual perpetrators are generally family members or trusted friends. Occasionally the perpetrator is a female, but that is not as common. Typical perpetrators may

be a father, stepfather, uncle, boyfriend, male cousin, or male neighbor. Sleepovers at a friend's home usually have male family members present, so sleepovers can be risky events for children.

- If the sleepover has lots of children in attendance, it is even riskier, because it is easy for one child to get separated from the group.
- Sleepovers leave children vulnerable to unfamiliar people. You and your child may not know all the children who are attending, nor do their parents. And you'll have no control over others who might "drop in" either.
- Sleepovers probably also will allow your children to have access to smartphones, tablets, computers, and television. Other families may not have the same standards you have about what your child can watch, but even if they do, during a sleepover it may not be possible for adults to provide enough supervision to monitor access to technology.

Should You Let Your Kids Attend Sleepovers?

Now that you are aware of the risks, you have to decide for yourself just how many risks you're willing to take. Here are some questions to ask yourself:

1. Are your children old enough to recognize when someone is trying to engage them in inappropriate sexual behavior? The younger your child, the greater the risk when you let them attend a sleepover. Younger children won't recognize a risky situation until it is too late.
2. Are your children assertive enough to draw attention to inappropriate overtures from other children or adults? Some

117

children have the confidence to yell or push away someone who's making them feel uncomfortable, while other children are too timid to try to stop an adult or older child from hurting them. No child should attend a sleepover who lacks the confidence and assertiveness to rebuff inappropriate sexual behavior.

3. Will your children call you if something unsafe is happening at a sleepover? Some children are easily influenced by peers and won't tell parents if something goes wrong.

4. How many children will be attending the sleepover? A sleepover with more than eight children per adult supervisor is too large. When calculating a ratio of one adult to eight children, the count must include all the children who will be in the house at the time of the sleepover.

5. Another issue to consider is the tensions that might arise with your children and other parents if you allow your children to go to sleepovers with some friends but not others. It's much easier to have a "no sleepovers" rule, without exceptions or individual explanations.

One compromise might be to allow your children to go to a sleepover until it is bedtime. You can allow your children to go and spend the evening, but then pick them up at 10:00 p.m., which will limit their vulnerability. Another alternative is to host the sleepover at your house, with sufficient and appropriate supervision.

Preparing Your Children for Sleepovers—or Not

If you are going to let your children attend sleepovers, they must have the language to talk about their bodies and safety. By age five, your children should understand what their private parts are and how to tell you if other people are touching their private parts. Refer back to the section titled "Children Five and Under: What They Should Know" and make sure you've discussed those issues with your children.

Above all, make sure your child knows that you will come immediately—day or any hour of the night—and take them home if they are the slightest bit uncomfortable. Tell them you want them to exercise their warrior heart by saying "NO!" to anything that "gives them the creeps," "makes their skin crawl," "is yucky," or any other term your family uses for a situation or remark that makes them ill at ease.

If you opt not to allow your children to go to sleepovers—which is my strong recommendation—you need to explain to them that God has given you the responsibility to raise them to follow Him, and part of the responsibility of raising children is keeping them safe. Letting them go to another house where you don't know what will happen is not doing what God expects you to do. God expects you to be present as much as possible and keep your children safe.

Finally, learn to trust your gut feelings, and teach your children to trust theirs too! Often God communicates through these things, and in such cases, it's better to be safe than sorry. If someone seems a little off or a little too nice to your kids, trust yourself and keep your kids out of any situations where they would be alone with that person. I recommend the book *The Gift of Fear*, which describes people forgetting to trust their intuition in potentially dangerous situations and why it is important to listen to that spirit of discernment.

If you feel that someone who expresses interest in your child is weird or is giving you the heebie-jeebies or other such sensations—pay attention to those inner alerts! Many a parent can relate a story in which the Holy Spirit gave an impression or feeling of warning that later was shown to be valid and protective.

It's true that all people have value in God's eyes, and you can be polite and respectful to anyone. *But you don't have to allow them access to your children.*

Messages for Your Child

Keep nurturing that warrior heart. Kids can learn to safeguard themselves if you give them the tools. Keep telling them these protective truths:

1. Children have the right to say no to anyone who asks them to do anything painful, embarrassing, or wrong.
2. No one can touch them on the parts of the body covered by a bathing suit, and they should not touch anyone else in these private places.
3. They must tell you immediately if someone tells them to keep a secret or tries to threaten them or bribe them. Assure them repeatedly that you will always be glad to know that, and they will not be in trouble.
4. Children have the right to refuse to look at pictures or videos of other people naked or engaged in sexual activities.
5. If they find themselves alone with an adult or peer in an isolated area where others cannot see them or in an unfamiliar place, they need to leave the situation immediately.
6. Children need to be aware of peers or adults who make jokes about or talk about sexual information. Your children need to know that God created sex to be a special bond between men and women who are married. They need to tell you if peers or adults are joking about sexual content or talking about sexual information with them.

7. Children need to know that talking about sexual information with friends or viewing sexual content does not make them more grown up. Rather, talking about sexual information or viewing pornographic information will likely confuse them about God's plan for sex.

If You Suspect Abuse

There are warning signs of abuse that your child may display, but remember not all children who are being sexually abused will have these signs. These red flags are when children

1. exhibit behaviors that change drastically or they are emotional;
2. express an unusual interest in sexual subjects or completely avoid sexual topics;
3. avoid individuals for no apparent reason or don't want to participate in certain activities;
4. experience sleep disturbances, bedwetting, or soiling; or
5. isolate themselves, are depressed, and have suicidal thoughts.

While these are all symptoms of sexual abuse, no single symptom will confirm a child has been sexually abused. If your child is exhibiting one or more of these symptoms, talk with him or her to make sure your child has not been abused.

If you suspect your child has been sexually or physically abused, remember not to overreact emotionally in front of your child. Let the child know you want to keep him or her safe—that it's your job, and you want to do it.

Take your concerns to a doctor, a social worker, or the police. You don't have to know that your child is not safe, you just have to suspect it to seek out professional assistance. And of course, don't leave your child in the same situation if you are concerned about his or her safety.

11

Abuse by Peer/Authority Figure

Summer Camp

It was a scary situation with a good ending, but that good ending took a while to materialize.

When Paige, a high school teacher, came into my office in late spring, I was surprised to see her. She was a stable, savvy single mother, hyper-aware of child safety issues in her teaching job at an alternative high school whose students were all being held in the local detention center. Due to her training and her job experience, she did a good job training her own children, Ramona, age ten, and GG, age eleven, about how to recognize safe and unsafe situations.

She came to me with a dilemma. At her job, she'd made the acquaintance of a young man, Sean, who'd committed a sexual offense against a younger child. Of course, Paige was unable to share any such confidential information with anyone else because of privacy laws, and would never do so.

I could hardly believe my ears when Paige described the setting in which she next encountered Sean—on the staff roster of the week-long summer camp her own girls, Ramona and GG, planned to attend!

"Imagine how surprised I was to find that! My kids went to this camp the last two summers and loved it in the mountains," Paige told me. I thought of the wonderful facilities and fresh air, so unlike the flat plains where we live.

"I knew the camp was primarily staffed by high school students, which is pretty common for summer camps," Paige continued. "I thought I'd asked the right questions about the adult supervision of these teen workers, but I didn't think to ask how they vetted these older kids they hired. In fact, the camp director told me they did background checks, so I assumed everything was all right."

"So he managed to get on staff without anyone knowing his record?" I asked. The local organization that sponsored the camp needed to know, if that were the case. It was a nonprofit with a good reputation.

"I went to the camp director and asked some broad questions about the process of hiring the high school kids they use as counselors," she said. "At first he kept telling me not to worry, that they did background checks. I kept asking questions. I couldn't believe my ears when the director admitted that they allow students with criminal backgrounds to work there."

I'll admit I felt a bit of anger. "You're kidding. The director said he let them work around the other high school students? With the younger kids?"

"Of course I couldn't tell him I knew anything about Sean. I kept pressing the director with hypotheticals until he finally told me that students with a record could be hired but couldn't stay in the cabins with the elementary age kids. I guess he thought I'd be relieved, but when he told me the adults at camp would supervise an offender, I was pretty sure they didn't have the training to be able to do that. And I don't think there are that many adults there, anyway."

"No," I agreed, "to be effective, they'd have to be able to keep a sexual offender within eyesight at all times, day and night." Paige would know that from her own training. And I was pretty sure this camp couldn't do that.

"And another thing bothered me," Paige said. "I mean, if they let this kid come in 'under the radar' as a staff member, is he the only one? Could there be others?"

"And even if the juvenile with the conviction wasn't a sex offender," I added, "who's to say they haven't hired someone who sold drugs, or someone who has assaulted someone his own age?"

Paige spread her hands out in the universal sign of confusion and distress.

I shared her concern. We both knew that placing such a juvenile—one who had already offended against younger children—in a camp setting was asking for trouble. But it was one week until camp, and her girls had been looking forward to it all year.

"What do you think?" Paige asked. "One thing that's in our favor is that you and I know that it's rare for someone who has offended against boys to choose to start offending against girls."

I nodded slowly. She was right about that: Most sex offenders are attracted to a specific age and gender. I sat back, considering the situation. "That's your call, but if you go ahead with the camp plans, I can help you navigate that."

Because of her job experience and the fact that her girls were already aware of safe and unsafe situations, we decided to have her and the girls meet with me. We gave them even more specific instructions, such as checking on each other, not going into any bathroom or shower if only an adult or high school student was in there alone with them, and being wary of a counselor or adult promising favors or goodies.

What if that should happen? The girls knew what to do—get away from the situation, find a safe adult, and tell all the details. Meanwhile, I was pretty sure that Paige's probing questions of the director had made the camp staff much more vigilant toward Sean.

When Paige and I met together again the week after camp, she reported the girls had a safe and happy time at camp. Meanwhile, Paige had been busy writing to the board members of the nonprofit, expressing her concern about the way they screened candidates for teen counselors.

Even better, I got a letter from her a while later saying the board had indeed revised their procedures.

There would be no more "Seans" at that camp in the future.

What Is the Role of Forgiveness/Restoration in a Pedophile Situation?

God does not want us to put our children in danger. While we may muster up forgiveness for pedophiles, the reality is that most child sex offenders will struggle with their attraction to children for the rest of their lives. To my knowledge, pedophilia is not a curable condition, that is, not an attraction that changes.

Child sex offenders who are trying not to offend *do not want to have access to children* because they realize that being around children can trigger their sexual desires. As concerned brothers and sisters in Christ, we should not place pedophiles in situations where they have the temptation of access to children.

What You Should Know about Camp

Summer camp is an enjoyable rite of passage in many families that provides great experiences for most children. In fact, a significant number of people say that their salvation experience occurred at a Christian camp. In selecting a camp, keep in mind that the summer camp you attended has changed since you were a kid, so selecting the same camp you attended may not be the wisest choice.

1. *Check out the camp's reputation.* Employers check references before they hire someone, so research the camp as if you were an employer. Talk to parents and their children about their experiences with the camp. Ask questions about what children liked about the camp and what they didn't like. Find out if kids are expected to be in their beds and asleep at certain times and what happens if children aren't in bed at that time. If you don't know names of children and their parents that you can contact, the camp should be willing to supply these to you. If a camp won't provide these references to you, find another camp.

2. *Learn about the camp's staff policies.* All camp counselors should have a background check before they are hired to work with children. In addition, camps should have policies prohibiting staff members from any one-on-one time with children. Each cabin should have at least two adults sleeping in it every night. There should be no circumstances in which staff members are allowed to be alone with individual campers. The camp should demonstrate that it has policies that address the safety of children in regard to environment and people. In addition, there must be a plan for how to reach you in case of an emergency.

3. *Learn about the camp's discipline policies.* While this book is primarily about sexual abuse, you need to be sure that your children are emotionally and physically safe as well. The camp should have written discipline policies that

are available for you to read. You also want to know who is responsible for overseeing disciplinary actions at the camp and feel comfortable with this individual administering discipline for your children if needed.

4. *Check for accreditation.* A camp that is accredited by the American Camp Association has to meet three hundred health and safety standards. True, a camp can be safe without accreditation, and accredited camps may also lack safety, but there's a better chance that the camp is more aware of safety if it is accredited. Accredited camps are generally responsible organizations that take seriously the safety of their facilities and staff.

5. *Learn about the camp's safety protocol.* A part of the safety protocol is background checks. But the most important part of safety protocol is training camp employees. Camp employees should have CPR training and water safety training if there is a pool or lake at the camp. And all camp employees should be trained on how to recognize physical and sexual abuse and how children talk about it, and how to report suspected abuse. If you don't feel one hundred percent confident of the camp's safety protocol, cross that camp off your list.

6. *Don't allow adult-child relationships from camp to come home.* Camps routinely discourage or prohibit staff members from spending time with campers outside of camp. This prohibition is essential because camp staff members who have the opportunity to develop a close relationship with your child at camp are in a position to influence your children. A sexual predator uses such influence to "groom" victims by integrating himself into the lives of children, becoming someone they like and trust.

7. *Review the camp's policies and routines about contact
between older and younger campers.* Most parents don't
realize that approximately one-third of sex offenders are
themselves children or adolescents. Camps need to divide
children by age group and limit the access of older children to younger children. Just as children may trust adults,
younger children can look up to and be influenced and
manipulated by older peers. If interaction between different age groups is allowed at camp, the interactions need to
be closely supervised.

Many of us have wonderful memories of camp and the rites of
passage it provides through childhood and adolescence. We want
the same amazing experience for our children. Certainly, fear cannot
determine decisions about camp for our children, but we will make
those decisions using wise guidelines. With wisdom and caution, our
children can have a life-shaping experience at a safe summer camp.

Preparing Your Child

- Before you send your children to camp, make sure they
  know the difference between safe and unsafe touch and
  what to do if someone touches them in an unsafe way (see
  chapter 2).
- Remind your children that no one should ask them to keep
  secrets—secrets are unsafe.
- Remind your children that no matter what another child
  or adult tells them, they will never get into trouble for telling you if someone touches them inappropriately.
- Emphasize that it is not okay for an adult to want to
  spend time one-on-one with them. While it is difficult

to explain to children the dangers of "exclusive relationships" between adults and children, they need to know they are precious to their parents and precious to God. Find ways to tell children that they are unique and special, that God created them to fulfill a unique place in His kingdom. They should feel special because God created them and because we love them.

- Your children should not accept gifts from others without your knowledge and approval. Do some simple role-playing in which someone gives them gifts or compliments, and how they can graciously decline. Nothing can compare with the love God has for them and how much we love them.

- Teach your children to trust their instincts. Our brains process a lot more information than we have in our awareness. Intuition is based on such processing that happens without our focused attention. Developing a warrior heart means that they'll more easily recognize danger signs. If someone makes your children feel uncomfortable or seems creepy, they need to tell you or another trusted adult. Trust your children's intuition and instincts about their own safety and keep them away from such people.

- Before your children go to camp, develop a communication plan. You need to know how to contact them and they need to know how to contact you, day or night, especially if they don't feel safe. Communication between you and your child should be immediate and easy.

- Camps should not monitor or restrict contact between you and your child. If a camp monitors contact between campers and parents, find another camp for your child to attend.

Getting to go to camp signals to your children that you understand they are growing up. It's a big deal, and you should tell them so. They're making an important transition toward adulthood by being away from you, and you affirm your trust in them.

As the apostle Paul said, there are times to be a child and behaviors that go with being a child, but that doesn't last forever: "When I was a child, I talked like a child, I thought like a child, I reasoned like a child. But when I became an adult, I set aside childish ways" (1 Corinthians 13:11 NET).

The ways of an adult, or one becoming an adult, are the ways of a warrior heart. Help your children go into this new arena and move toward adulthood, and acknowledge that they are growing more independent and have better skills for protecting themselves.

Messages for Your Child

Keep nurturing that warrior heart. Kids can learn to safeguard themselves if you give them the tools. Keep telling them these protective truths:

1. Children have the right to say no to anyone who asks them to do anything painful, embarrassing, or wrong.
2. No one can touch them on the parts of the body covered by a bathing suit, and they should not touch anyone else in these private places.
3. They must tell you immediately if someone tells them to keep a secret or tries to threaten them or bribe them. Assure them repeatedly that you will always be glad to know that, and they will not be in trouble.

4. Children have the right to refuse to look at pictures or videos of other people naked or engaged in sexual activities.

5. If they find themselves alone with an adult or peer in an isolated area where others cannot see them or in an unfamiliar place, they need to leave the situation immediately.

6. Children need to be aware of peers or adults who make jokes about or talk about sexual information. Your children need to know that God created sex to be a special bond between men and women who are married. They need to tell you if peers or adults are joking about sexual content or talking about sexual information with them.

7. Children need to know that talking about sexual information with friends or viewing sexual content does not make them more grown up. Rather, talking about sexual information or viewing pornographic information will likely confuse them about God's plan for sex.

If You Suspect Abuse

There are warning signs of abuse that your child may display, but *remember not all children who are being sexually abused will have these signs*. These red flags are when children

1. exhibit behaviors that change drastically or they are emotional;

2. express an unusual interest in sexual subjects or completely avoid sexual topics;

3. avoid individuals for no apparent reason or don't want to participate in certain activities;

4. experience sleep disturbances, bedwetting, or soiling; or
5. isolate themselves, are depressed, and have suicidal thoughts.

While these are all symptoms of sexual abuse, no single symptom will confirm a child has been sexually abused. If your child is exhibiting one or more of these symptoms, talk with him or her to make sure your child has not been abused.

If you suspect your child has been sexually or physically abused, remember not to overreact emotionally in front of your child. Let the child know you want to keep him or her safe—that it's your job, and you want to do it.

Take your concerns to a doctor, a social worker, or the police. You don't have to know that your child is not safe, you just have to suspect it to seek out professional assistance. And of course, don't leave your child in the same situation if you are concerned about his or her safety.

12

Abuse by Stranger

Riding Bikes in the Neighborhood

Usually when a mother ends up in my office for a first consultation, she is crying or at least on the verge of tears. But when Lisa, who'd been referred to me by some mutual friends at her church, begins to talk, there are no tears.

"I have to give you some background," she says, describing front-porch life in the small town where she'd grown up, a place where everyone knew everyone and where people watched out for one another. After marriage, Lisa and her husband knew that was the safe place they wanted to raise their children.

I ask about her children, and I try to interpret the different facial expressions—ranging from pride to tenderness to something else, as she describes her ten-year-old daughter, Sydney, and her eight-year-old son, Sam.

Now as she talks, anger seems to rise off her round face like steam.

"I've known our neighbors, Joe and Joanne, my whole life," she says. "So when I found out their grandson from Phoenix was going to be moving in with them, I wanted him to feel welcome."

"What is the grandson's name?" I ask, and she almost spits out the answer.

"Tyson."

I wait until she composes herself.

"He didn't know anyone in our town, so he spent most of his time with my kids. I should have been more concerned, I guess, when Tyson—he's thirteen—didn't seem to click with older kids, but since everybody was always playing outside, I wasn't worried." She looks up at me, defensive. "But I always tried to make sure I could see them out the window, riding bikes or playing in the yard."

"Yes."

"Then one day Sydney came running into the house, screaming at the top of her lungs that Tyson was holding Sam down on the ground. By the time I got to the corner of the yard, I could see Sam facedown on the grass with his pants pulled down. Tyson was on top of him, with his hand over Sam's mouth."

I ask the next question delicately. "What happened after that?"

"I grabbed both my kids and took them home. They both told me this was the first time Tyson had done anything like this, and we figured out that after Sam's pants were down, nothing else had happened. I was still furious—but then I realized I was scaring my kids, so I sent them in to watch television until my husband, Brett, came home."

"How did he react?" I ask.

"We were both glad I got to Tyson when I did—who knows what would have happened if I hadn't?" She is shaking. "At first we thought we should call the police, but we decided to call Child Protective Services."

"What did they say?"

"They said since nothing actually happened, it was a low priority and they weren't sure when—or even if—they would investigate it. Brett and I were exhausted by that time, so we decided to pray about it and wait until the morning to call Tyson's grandparents."

"How did they respond?"

"Well, we told them we needed to come over and discuss something. We got a sitter and went over that night. As soon as I told them what I'd seen Tyson doing, Joanne started crying and saying, 'Oh no, oh no, it was true.'"

"What did she mean by that?"

"It finally came out that Joe and Joanne had Tyson living with them because CPS was investigating what Adam, Tyson's six-year-old brother, had told one of his teachers—that Tyson had been playing what he called 'private parts games' with him. After an investigation, CPS said that Tyson had to be in a home with no other kids."

"And so he ended up with his grandparents and in your neighborhood," I say. She nods. "And without any close supervision. And putting other kids at risk."

"Jim and Joanne said he didn't have a phone or video games, so they thought getting a bike and riding around the neighborhood would be a safe thing," she says. "And I ignored that funny feeling I had about my kids playing with someone outside their age group. Now I am nervous and irritable all the time. I don't want to let my kids out of my sight. I just don't know what to do."

While it is understandable that Lisa wanted to keep her children in her sight at all times and was exhausting herself trying to monitor her children 24/7, the reality is that a few strategies can help you monitor your children's safety without constant eyesight supervision. One of the easiest changes to make is to change your own location when you are supervising your children.

If your children are outside riding bikes, can you sit on the front porch? If you are doing something inside your home that you can do sitting outside, go outside! If you are folding laundry, can you fold it on the porch, and go in and out of the house just to transfer wet clothes to the dryer? If you are cooking, you can sometimes restructure your meals or meal times, or use an Instapot or Crock-Pot so you can stay outside.

If you are engaged in activities where you cannot provide supervision outside, you should probably be doing eyesight check-ins with your children approximately every fifteen minutes if they are out in the neighborhood. Or better yet, bring them inside when you are cooking and let them help you prepare the meal and learn to cook at the same time.

If your children want to play with friends, invite their friends to your house rather than having your children go to friends' houses. Make your house the home where all the kids in the neighborhood want to come to and spend time.

How can you do that? Decide to put on a "welcome" face when you see their friends. Grit your teeth when they track in dirt. Ask about their sports activities, or favorite team, or dolls or other toys. Get to know them.

Provide snacks and water and drinks for them, out in the open so they don't have to ask. Decide that a messy kitchen is a small price to pay for the rewards of having kids mix and bake cookies, for instance.

Watch at garage sales and thrift stores for board games that your kids will like to play—activities that will keep them together, and in your sight. Get a basketball hoop or other equipment for group games in your backyard where you can see them.

In your home, you can provide the supervision of your children and their friends. Have the same rules for children as you would for adults in your home. When you have guests, you generally spend time with your friends in the shared spaces in your home such as the living room, the kitchen, the den, or the dining room. Similarly, we should expect our children to stay in the shared spaces in our homes, not in bedrooms, when they have friends over.

It Happens in Your Neighborhood

We feel safer and less vulnerable when we believe there are some locations that will always be safe for our children or people they will always be safe with.

I want to be clear that *there are no absolutely safe places*. That doesn't mean every place is unsafe. It just means that you need to be aware of warning signs and provide good supervision. You don't have to be paranoid, just thoughtful and smart.

When we accept the fact that sexual abuse of children could happen in our neighborhood, it shifts our thinking. We pay more attention to what our children and other people are doing in the neighborhood. We stay off our phones when we are in the park. We let our children play in our own backyard if we can't provide supervision in other parts of the neighborhood.

We don't walk around scared. We walk around aware.

Check the Sex Offender Registry

I hate to tell you this: The overwhelming majority of sex offenders will not be caught, prosecuted, and convicted. But you should pay attention to the registry of those who are. The research is clear that most sex offenders perpetrate many times before the first time they are caught or accused. So if someone gets caught and convicted, he or she likely has assaulted before and therefore should be viewed as a threat to your children.

You can go online and find a registry of convicted sex offenders through your local law enforcement agency. In researching this chapter, I did such a search for the county where my elderly mother lives. I was surprised to discover that a convicted child sex offender lives within a block of my mother's house! I looked at his picture and thought that if I had seen him in my mom's neighborhood and he had stopped and offered to help me with something, I would have accepted the help. In his picture, he is clean-cut; he looks safe.

Take a look at the sex offender registry for your area to identify how the perpetraters in your area look. Some of them are scruffy-looking characters—but not all! You'll find there is no single characteristic that would let you identify a sex offender. It's not always their looks. You have to be aware of the *behaviors* of sex offenders in order to protect your children.

You Don't Know the History of Other Kids

A concept we haven't discussed yet is your assumptions about other children. We tend to assume that children growing up in the same schools and churches with our kids have the same kind of background. But for many reasons, caregivers or parents often do not reveal to others that the children in their care may have problematic sexual behavior.

I worked with two elementary age brothers whom our state's Child Protective Services had removed and placed in a shelter. The brothers had been abused in their mother's home and were engaging in problematic sexual behaviors with other children.

Child Protective Services located the father of the two boys. He was financially stable and had a safe home, but because the mother of his boys had kept them away from him, he was unaware of the removal of his sons or their abuse.

The father was eager to parent his sons and believed that if his sons came to live with him and were away from their mother and the abuse, there would be no problematic sexual behaviors. He was naïve, but his intentions were good.

Six weeks after the boys were placed with their father, the school called their father and reported that the son in first grade had anally penetrated a kindergarten student in the school bathroom. After further investigation, school personnel discovered that both brothers had been acting out sexually with other students in the bathroom at school.

The two brothers were in the first and second grade at a public school in an affluent neighborhood. They were well dressed, neatly groomed, and well behaved, except for the sexual behaviors. If you, as a parent, had met these boys, you would not have immediately worried about your children playing with them.

Remember, you never know the background and experience of children who have not been in your home since birth.

What to Teach Your Kids

Set clear family guidelines for personal privacy and behavior. Discuss them with all members of your family and model respecting these guidelines. Make it plain that these are not things you're ashamed of—you have a warrior heart, and you want your house to be a place where warrior hearts learn, love, and play.

Of course, this is a fluid process as your child matures. Rules will certainly change. Even you must respect his or her personal boundaries by knocking before entering your child's room, for instance.

Discuss these guidelines with any other adults who spend time around or supervise the children. For instance, it's okay if a child does not want to hug or kiss someone hello or good-bye—he or she can shake hands instead.

Let children know that if they are not comfortable being around a particular adult or older child, then you or another adult will let that person know this. You take the lead on behalf of your child and tell the adult that, for instance, you don't want your child sitting in any adult's lap. Or tell the older child, "We don't play in the bedrooms in this house."

Would it surprise you to know that even Jesus was cautious in trusting the people He was around? It's true. He knew the sad reality that not all people are what they seem to be. "But Jesus would not entrust himself to them, for he knew all people. He did not need any testimony about mankind, for he knew what was in each person" (John 2:24–25).

If the Savior of the world was selective and cautious about relationships, how much more you and your children should be!

Messages for Your Child

Keep nurturing that warrior heart. Kids can learn to safeguard themselves if you give them the tools. Keep telling them these protective truths:

1. Children have the right to say no to anyone who asks them to do anything painful, embarrassing, or wrong.
2. No one can touch them on the parts of the body covered by a bathing suit, and they should not touch anyone else in these private places.
3. They must tell you immediately if someone tells them to keep a secret or tries to threaten them or bribe them.

Assure them repeatedly that you will always be glad to know that, and they will not be in trouble.

4. Children have the right to refuse to look at pictures or videos of other people naked or engaged in sexual activities.

5. If they find themselves alone with an adult or peer in an isolated area where others cannot see them or in an unfamiliar place, they need to leave the situation immediately.

6. Children need to be aware of peers or adults who make jokes about or talk about sexual information. Your children need to know that God created sex to be a special bond between men and women who are married. They need to tell you if peers or adults are joking about sexual content or talking about sexual information with them.

7. Children need to know that talking about sexual information with friends or viewing sexual content does not make them more grown up. Rather, talking about sexual information or viewing pornographic information will likely confuse them about God's plan for sex.

If You Suspect Abuse

There are warning signs of abuse that your child may display, but *remember not all children who are being sexually abused will have these signs.* These red flags are when children

1. exhibit behaviors that change drastically or they are emotional;

2. express an unusual interest in sexual subjects or completely avoid sexual topics;

3. avoid individuals for no apparent reason or don't want to participate in certain activities;

4. experience sleep disturbances, bedwetting, or soiling; or

5. isolate themselves, are depressed, and have suicidal thoughts.

While these are all symptoms of sexual abuse, no single symptom will confirm a child has been sexually abused. If your child is exhibiting one or more of these symptoms, talk with him or her to make sure your child has not been abused.

If you suspect your child has been sexually or physically abused, remember not to overreact emotionally in front of your child. Let the child know you want to keep him or her safe—that's your job, and you want to do it.

Take your concerns to a doctor, a social worker, or the police. You don't have to know that your child is not safe, you just have to suspect it to seek out professional assistance. And of course, don't leave your child in the same situation if you are concerned about his or her safety.

13

Abuse Involving Technology
The Wikipedia Ambush

Sometimes you can do everything right and still encounter a problem. But the story of what happened to nine-year-old Andrew shows how good training and communication can save the day.

Andrew is a good kid who was waylaid by one bad situation after another. His grandparents, Ray and Sally, were raising him after their daughter, a single mom, was incarcerated for drug use. Ray and Sally were determined not to make the mistakes they had made with their daughter. They took Andrew to church, attended parenting classes, and read books and articles about how to keep Andrew safe and help him develop into a responsible Christian man.

Being a part of a church community helped them, even though most of the other parents were younger. They participated in the children's program, often hosted parties for kids at their home, and sought the advice of others when they encountered challenges.

And so it was that after church on a Wednesday night, Ray and Sally stopped me to talk about Andrew and his technology use.

Like most wise parents, they keep the computer and gaming system in the living room so they can see what Andrew accesses on the computer. Even though it was difficult for them, they got themselves "up to speed" on new technologies and talked to Andrew about how to use them responsibly.

They had discussed pornography with him, initiating conversations about how sex was intended to occur in marriage between a husband and a wife, and that viewing sex on media or reading about it in books was something they would always need to discuss.

They wanted to equip Andrew to make good decisions about what to watch on television, and they set standards of what movie ratings were appropriate for him. Sometimes, though, even PG-rated movies had violence or profanity or themes they weren't comfortable with. One day Andrew heard about a movie from friends at school and Sally suggested he look it up online to see its rating.

One of the first listings about the movie on Google was a Wikipedia entry. As Andrew looked at the movie description, he clicked on the director's name, which led him to another listing. In that listing, it mentioned that the director had filmed a "money shot." Curious about the meaning of that seemingly innocuous term, Andrew clicked on that.

"He came running out of the living room to the kitchen where I was cooking dinner," Sally said to me. "He was so upset—red in the face, looking like he was about to cry."

"I didn't mean to do it!" he began. "I tried to get rid of it!"

Andrew hung back when Sally approached the family computer. She saw on the screen several explicit line drawings of sexual acts. Because Andrew was already so upset and distressed, she turned off the computer screen and then walked him over to the couch.

Sally put her arm around his shoulder and reassured him he wasn't in trouble. "You came and got me right away," she told him. "Good job! You knew what to do!"

She kept reassuring him that he wasn't in trouble, and asked questions about how he ended up on that site.

"It was the movie the other kids were talking about," Andrew said. "The movie looked kind of stupid and was just about people fighting and gambling." But the movie description used a term he didn't know: *money shot*. He thought the term referred to shooting a gun a certain way and was shocked when the hyperlink led him to line drawings of ejaculation and an article filled with further hyperlinks to graphic line drawings of other sexual acts.

Again, Andrew's grandmother assured him he'd not done anything wrong. In fact, she assured him he had done something *really right* by coming to tell her. She sent him off to play and checked the browsing history of the computer. What Andrew told her was supported by the browser history. He'd just stumbled onto the site.

I suggested that Sally and Ray come to my office to discuss this a little further.

We spent most of our time together talking about how to talk to Andrew about the line drawings he saw on the computer. I suggested at least one follow-up conversation with Andrew to make sure he didn't have any misperceptions. My major concern was that Andrew understand that God created sex and that sex is a great thing in a marriage. Sometimes when kids are corrected for looking at sexual images or listening to sexually inappropriate music, we inadvertently send the message that sex itself is bad.

Andrew's grandparents have a unique opportunity to teach him about how God created sex to be a special bond and connection between a husband and a wife. When people engage in sex outside of marriage, they often get hurt emotionally or hurt others because they create a connection and then break the connection.

Sex is created by God and is good, and our children need to hear that from us.

Even for obedient kids like Andrew whose parents are vigilant, online porn can ambush them. It's everywhere, and Wikipedia is one of the worst places. You should have a rule for your children (as do most schools) that Wikipedia cannot be used in school assignments. Ever. Even though an informational item may be quite harmless, it may contain links—or links to links—that can lead a kid right into porn.

The same is true of the most popular site of all for children and teens, YouTube. There are thousands of informative, funny, and how-to videos there. Though YouTube claims to prohibit porn, they don't often regulate porn and links in the comments sections. One click and you're looking at things you never wanted to see.

Andrew exemplified behavior mentioned in an account in the Bible. In fact, I wouldn't be surprised if his grandparents had told him about Joseph, a young man in the Old Testament who was also ambushed by a sexual situation. Handsome Joseph had to fend off continual sneaky sexual harassment from his boss's wife. One day, when he was minding his own business and taking care of his boss's property, he went inside and found, to his horror, that he was alone in the house with the lusty wife. He fought her off when she attacked him and she grabbed his garment when he ran outside.

Sometimes you can't think your way through a bad situation. Sometimes, like Joseph, you just have to run from it; that's what Andrew did. We have to teach our children that not all enemies should be engaged in battle. If they are going to "flee from sexual immorality" as 1 Corinthians 6:18 says, it may involve literally running away.

Your anti-spyware software may keep your family off porn sites and other dangerous spam sites, but if not, you may have to invest in accountability software such as Covenant Eyes, or download a browser or app that blocks porn—there are many of these from which to choose.

Such "safe browsers" provide protection against unwanted sexual content. They also can protect your home and your credit rating! They can keep an innocent kid from clicking on innocuous or funny links that compromise the computer's safety—and turn over passwords to your bank accounts and other assets.

Technology opens the door (sometimes literally) and invites strangers you may not want your children to know into your living room, into the bedrooms of your home. Here's a safe bet: A large number of strangers who come into your home via the Internet may have the exact opposite goals for your children as you do. Where you want to nurture and protect, they want to sully and isolate. If nothing else moves you, imagine all you've written or posted about your child in the last month, printed out and in the hands of a delighted predator.

There are several reasons why we must actively and overtly monitor our children's access to the Internet through technology. Because of predators, yes. But we also want to prevent our children from giving out personal information that could be used to target them or our families in any manner of intimidating or bullying ways. Personal information in the hands of a criminal can put you and your child in physical danger.

Unfortunately, our own carelessness often combines with the innocence of children's hearts, and we reveal more about our children and their whereabouts than any stranger should know. We don't think—and kids certainly don't think—that they are giving out personal information such as their house number behind them in a back-to-school photo, for example. But even without a house number, a determined predator can extract the metadata from a photo and use it to determine a location. What can you do? Strip the metadata from any photos you or your child post.[1]

In addition to some of the obvious ways we want to protect our children, there are important advantages to monitoring our children's use of technology. Their digital conversations will help us learn about their friends. We can help steer our children away from peers who may influence them in inappropriate ways. I have experienced with great sadness the cyberbullying that has become part of the fabric of our children's world. But through monitoring digital access, our spiritual and protective antennae will activate if someone starts to bully our children online—or if our children start bullying other children.

Children need us to teach them how to interact with other people. Sometimes we may not realize that teaching about relationships (what used to be called "manners" and other kind and reciprocal aspects of relationships) extends to digital relationships today. Teach your child the signs of bullying; talk about them at the dinner table or in the car (great information is available at StopBullying.gov, for instance).

In addition, we also need to teach our children that some information is too personal to be exposed online to other people. Once information has been posted online, it is impossible to remove it. It is like the old moral story about the girl who had spread gossip and was sorry about it. A wise old person told her to go out at night and lay a feather on the doorstep of each person she'd talked to or about. The next morning, of course, the feathers had blown to the four winds. The same is true of anything posted on the Internet. It is immortal. It will never go away, and you can never take it back.

One way to explain privacy issues to a child is to ask, "Would you like for someone to have a key to your house and be able to take your favorite toys and turn them into sculptures in a park far, far away?" Any time a young person posts a revealing picture, they are handing out keys to their own privacy. Sometimes kids post things they think make them look older or more daring than they are. Keep a close eye on what your child posts.

Our children may also be targeted by viruses and malware or have their identities stolen online when they give out private information. Thieves troll the Internet looking for such things so they can steal identities for fake IDs to open credit card accounts, or commit other kinds of fraud.

Adults fall victim to such scams every day. Certainly children do not have the ability to evaluate the trustworthiness of a person, a site, or a download.

Our job as parents is to walk with our children on a digital journey and help them navigate a digital world with healthy boundaries that protect them and others online.

Strategies for Monitoring Technology

- *Limit screen time.* The easiest way to monitor technology is to limit screen time. The less time our children are online, the less we have to monitor. Research demonstrates that children are healthier and happier with less screen time and more active play and thinking time. Pediatricians recommend limiting screen time (any interaction with technology) to two hours a day.

- *Keep technology in shared rooms.* Locating the television and computer in the living room will allow you to easily monitor what your children are seeing. That will bring your children into shared areas rather than allowing them to hibernate in the rooms with technology. This is a win-win, because our kids get to interact with us more, and we prefer they learn from us rather than from strangers online.

- *Let technology rest.* When your children are young is the perfect time to teach them boundaries about technology, boundaries that are easier to reinforce as they grow. All devices need a bedtime. When kids go to sleep, they leave their devices with you so you can charge the devices. You can create an area for all the technology at night where you can charge it and monitor it. (Of course, as a good role model, you will want to put your technology away at night and let it recharge. What's good for your kids is even better for you.)

- *Monitor your safety filter.* Add safety filters to most technology devices. Some of the safety filters are called parental controls. These allow you to set what types of information your children can access on their devices. However, our children are frequently smarter than we are in regard to technology and learn to bypass safety filters faster than we learn to install them. Regularly check the filters and spot-check what your children are accessing to make sure the filters are working. Change passwords often.

- *Install monitoring software.* Monitoring software for computers, tablets, and phones lets you know exactly what your children are viewing and what they are sending in their messages and emails by tracking key strokes. While some parents may argue that they don't want to spy on their children, I believe this is not spying but rather providing the same type of protection online that we would provide in face-to-face interactions. If you begin using monitoring software when your children are young, they will be much more accepting of it when they are teenagers, growing up believing that monitoring software is just part of using technology.

Remember an important fact that your children need to hear come out of your mouth early and often: You are the parent in the home and you set the rules about the use of technology. You pay for the Wi-Fi. You pay the cell phone and Internet bills. Even if a friend or relative gives your child an electronic device (including game players that can often communicate on the Internet), you set the rules about the use of the device and when children will have access to the device. Your children must know they can use them only when, where, and how you say. You can restrict use of technology at any time. (And don't be afraid to lock away the devices they misuse. Make this a priority in your home.)

Reactions to Inappropriate Information

Perhaps the most important component in teaching your children about safety and technology is how you react when (not if!) your children access inappropriate information either intentionally or unintentionally. Your reaction to their lapses will open many more opportunities to teach them, if you handle the situations with grace and calmness.

This is a process. Nobody learns how to be an adult all at once. We teach little by little as children grow and mature and earn more freedom in how to interact appropriately. We take the mistakes and lapses of our children and help them learn how to interact in a different way online. The next time, we assure them, they will be smarter.

There is no value in humiliating our children if they make mistakes. Instead, we should encourage them to be honest, and we should demonstrate to them that we will be supportive of them when they are in difficult situations.

It can seem overwhelming for parents and kids to try to anticipate and deal with all the dangers that the world wants to throw at us. Even if you start out with innocent motives, like Andrew and his grandparents did, you can find yourself in a bad situation before you even know what happened.

The Ambush Nature of Temptation

Latayne told her children about temptation: "It's like how I used to catch squirrels when I was a kid. I'd prop up an upside-down lidless box with a stick, and attach a string to the stick. On the ground under the box, I'd put some bread or something else to tempt the squirrel, who would cautiously enter, its nose twitching with anticipation. But I'd pull the string, and boom! The box would drop and the squirrel would be inside.

"That's the way some temptations happen. You're just looking, just smelling, and boom! You're trapped.

"But there's good news! First Corinthians 10:13 tells us a secret about temptation. All temptations have an escape hatch: 'No temptation has overtaken you except what is common to mankind. And God is faithful; he will not let you be tempted beyond what you can bear. But when you are tempted, he will also provide a way out so that you can endure it.'"

Tell your children this important truth: *There is no inescapable temptation.* For every temptation they face, God has built into it, as one of its essential features, the way to get out of it.

Tell your kids when they are ambushed to feel around in the dark of the box to find the door that is surely there.

Tell them, "Run if you have to! There's always a door that will open when you find it."

Messages for Your Child

Keep nurturing that warrior heart. Kids can learn to safeguard themselves if you give them the tools. Keep telling them these protective truths:

1. Children have the right to say no to anyone who asks them to do anything painful, embarrassing, or wrong.

2. No one can touch them on the parts of the body covered by a bathing suit, and they should not touch anyone else in these private places.

3. They must tell you immediately if someone tells them to keep a secret or tries to threaten them or bribe them. Assure them repeatedly that you will always be glad to know that, and they will not be in trouble.

4. Children have the right to refuse to look at pictures or videos of other people naked or engaged in sexual activities.

5. If they find themselves alone with an adult or peer in an isolated area where others cannot see them or in an unfamiliar place, they need to leave the situation immediately.

6. Children need to be aware of peers or adults who make jokes about or talk about sexual information. Your children need to know that God created sex to be a special bond between men and women who are married. They need to tell you if peers or adults are joking about sexual content or talking about sexual information with them.

7. Children need to know that talking about sexual information with friends or viewing sexual content does not make them more grown up. Rather, talking about sexual information or viewing pornographic information will likely confuse them about God's plan for sex.

If You Suspect Abuse

There are warning signs of abuse that your child may display, but *remember not all children who are being sexually abused will have these signs.* These red flags are when children

1. exhibit behaviors that change drastically or they are emotional;
2. express an unusual interest in sexual subjects or completely avoid sexual topics;
3. avoid individuals for no apparent reason or don't want to participate in certain activities;
4. experience sleep disturbances, bedwetting, or soiling; or
5. isolate themselves, are depressed, and have suicidal thoughts.

While these are all symptoms of sexual abuse, no single symptom will confirm a child has been sexually abused. If your child is exhibiting one or more of these symptoms, talk with him or her to make sure your child has not been abused.

If you suspect your child has been sexually or physically abused, remember not to overreact emotionally in front of your child. Let the child know you want to keep him or her safe—that it's your job, and you want to do it.

Take your concerns to a doctor, a social worker, or the police. You don't have to know that your child is not safe, you just have to suspect it to seek out professional assistance. And of course, don't leave your child in the same situation if you are concerned about his or her safety.

Ages Twelve and Older

14

Ages Twelve and Older
What Your Adolescent Should Know

I f you have teenagers, you know that sexual safety for teens ramps up and is more complicated than sexual safety for children. But this safety has a foundation as outlined in previous "What They Should Know" sections, and by the time someone reaches age twelve they should already

- know the specific names for male and female genitalia;
- know the difference between a safe touch (as from a doctor) and an unsafe one;
- know that no one can touch their genitalia or breasts without permission;
- feel confident that parents will listen to and support them if they feel they have been sexually violated or threatened; and
- know how and why to resist being bribed, threatened, or manipulated by a predator of any age, gender, or position of authority.

Refresh your skills and make sure your children know the information that deals with the age group younger than your children.

Some of this is covered in sex education classes, but they tend to focus on sexually transmitted diseases and pregnancy rather than understanding sexuality. Even the best secular sex education classes only describe the biology of sex, not the connection and spirituality of sexuality. For teens to be truly safe, they have to understand sexuality from a biblical perspective.

Tell your kids God isn't doing damage control on unmanageable hormones by giving us rules to restrict sex. He *invented* sex. Sex is normal. It was part of His plan and was in His mind when He created a male gender and a female one. It's private and sacred, but it's not shameful.

God heartily approves of sex! And not just so that the human race can keep reproducing, but so a man and his wife can lavishly enjoy each other. If you don't think that's God's attitude, you haven't read the Song of Solomon lately.

The Bond

God created the sexual relationship to unbreakably bond a man and a woman together for the rest of their lives. A neurochemical in women called oxytocin creates trust and bonding. When a woman is hugged for as little as twenty seconds, oxytocin is released and the woman begins to trust and bond. Touching, gazing, positive emotional interaction, kissing, and sexual interactions also release oxytocin in a woman's brain. This release creates an addictive craving for more oxytocin. Women are created to seek more physical intimacy, which leads to a stronger bond and trust in their partner.

Similarly, men have a neurochemical in their brains called vasopressin, which leads them to bond with their wives and their children. That's when bonding works as it was designed.

So quite literally, men and women attach to every person they have sex with. However, the ability to attach is like tape that loses its stickiness after being applied and removed multiple times. Similarly, when teens of both genders engage in sexual relationships, it damages the brain's ability to attach and desensitizes the brain to the risks of short-term relationships.

It can hurt. When even a short-term relationship breaks up, it is felt in the same brain centers as physical pain and can be seen on brain scans. On the other hand, the bonding process can also be short-circuited so that couples progress immediately to having sex.

You don't have to threaten consequences for teens who engage in sexual behavior—the consequences are built in, and you can discuss the research with your kids.

- People who are not virgins when they marry are more likely to divorce than those who remain abstinent until marriage.[1]
- Sexually active adolescents are more likely to be depressed than adolescents who abstain.[2]
- Married couples report higher levels of sexual satisfaction than do unmarried individuals with multiple sexual partners.

If teens know that sexual activity is a process, not a culminating event, they're more able to identify when behaviors of others may be inappropriate, and when they themselves can be sending signals unaware. While the whole thing is thrilling (you do remember your first sexual awarenesses, right?), they need help in knowing what makes certain behaviors suggestive—and can get them into dangerous situations. Because boys and girls are wired differently, girls are often completely unaware of how immediately a visual stimulus can arouse a boy. However, girls need to know that it is never their "fault" when a male coerces them into a sexual encounter.

Media and our current culture have a strong influence on teens, and they can also provide opportunities to create a dialogue with our teens about sexual behaviors. First, we can help them look around at others and see how different media situations are from real life. Once that's established, you can ask them how the actors and other personalities exerted or experienced sexual pressure and how that could be short-circuited or prevented. Furthermore, some media situations that turn out to be dangerous or disastrous can also be a good topic for discussion by asking questions such as, "At what point could she have stopped this situation?" "If you rewind to the point where she's making bad decisions, what advice would you give her?" "Who could help her in this situation?"

Strategies

While teens are trying to develop adult independence, it is important to teach them the difference between being independent and engaging in dangerous behaviors.

- At this age, it is important to teach your children to not only be wisely wary of older teens and adults, but also to stay together with friends in groups, and to never wander off—to explore or even to vent.

- One essential behavior that all teenagers should become experts in is to never enter a public bathroom or go shopping on their own—and to never leave a store or other public place with a stranger.
- Help your teens recognize that they don't have enough life experience to recognize when people are trying to lure them into dangerous situations.
- Teach your children that drugs and alcohol dull their judgment so they have less ability to discern what is safe and what is unsafe. Even further danger is posed by date-rape drugs—by peers putting drugs or alcohol in drinks. Encourage vigilance whenever your child accepts any beverage.

Talking Points

All teens mature differently, and some may feel pressured to behave in more sexualized ways than they're comfortable with. In this case, reassure your child that it is completely normal to be less interested in sex than their peers may be. Discuss with them the dangers of sexual pressures and possible scenarios involving risky behaviors that they do not wish to participate in. Again, being open with your teens about real-life situations will help them understand the dangers and be more willing to ask and answer questions with you.

Look at the flip side of the coin too. Did you know that U.S. Treasury agents teach their newbies to recognize counterfeit bills by first carefully studying the features of authentic currency? Similarly, you can direct your child toward healthy sexual attitudes and safe behavior by pointing them to successful marriages and other thriving, godly relationships.

But what if you're a single parent? Or have a difficult or uncooperative spouse? Though your own marriage may not have ideal characteristics, seek out the company of those whose marriages do, especially older couples, and let your kids see how it's done.

You can help keep teens safe from predators by repeatedly assuring them it is safe to talk to you. Listen more and talk less. The more you listen, the better you will understand your teens; it will show your teens that you are concerned and interested in them.

Practice asking open-ended questions rather than questions that will get a "yes" or "no" answer, or questions to which you already know the answer. Need a prompt? Ask questions that begin with the word *How* . . . That allows teens to respond with information.

When you are talking with your teens, keep your conversations respectful. If we treat them with respect rather than embarrassing, criticizing, or lecturing them, they will learn how to have respectful conversations with us and others.

You can reflect the feelings and ideas of your teens by rewording what they say to assure them and yourself that you understand. We don't have to agree with them, but by acknowledging what they are saying and feeling, we are helping our teens understand we are really listening.

Good conversations don't just happen—we have to create both time and space for our teens to talk with us. Seek out and plan for one-on-one activities with your teen. Sometimes it's easier for teens to talk to us when they are engaged in an activity and don't have to look directly at us, as when riding in a car or walking.

Strengthening a warrior heart in a teen is challenging, because that heart has so many demands for its attention. It's a time of great emotional highs and lows—for parents and kids alike.

But we have a Savior who likewise knew the depths of great emotion. One time when He saw a crowd of helpless, harassed people, He felt deep emotion—in fact, the Greek word indicates

He felt it in His gut (Matthew 9:36). It was overwhelming. So much to be done; so few who knew what to do.

> Jesus went through all the towns and villages, teaching in their synagogues, proclaiming the good news of the kingdom and healing every disease and sickness. When he saw the crowds, he had compassion on them, because they were harassed and helpless, like sheep without a shepherd. Then he said to his disciples, "The harvest is plentiful but the workers are few. Ask the Lord of the harvest, therefore, to send out workers into his harvest field."
>
> Matthew 9:35–38

Jesus knows firsthand how high the stakes are for you and your children, and He hears and helps.

15

Abuse by Authority Figure

The Mission Trip

When sixteen-year-old Julie stops me in the hallway at church, I can tell she is very upset. Julie, who had a difficult childhood, had been adopted by a young couple at church who seem to be doing a great job in their new role, and I hadn't seen the teenager as a client for several years.

"Do you need to see me in counseling or do you just need a few minutes?" I ask her.

Julie motions toward a section of the church foyer where nobody is standing. "Just a few minutes," she says, then adds, "This isn't about me, but I don't know what to do.

"I've got a friend, Sarah," she begins after we relocate. "She doesn't go to this church, but she's a Christian. A great Christian, as a matter of fact." Julie wrings her hands, and I wait for her to decide how to tell me what's on her mind.

"Sarah showed me some text messages between her and her youth minister. They didn't seem . . . right."

"How's that?"

"Well, they sound like a couple. Almost like dating, I guess."

"How did you respond when you saw these texts?"

"Well, you know about the abuse in my biological family. These texts just reminded me of that. It gave me the creeps. I didn't know what to say, but she could see I didn't like it either."

"How can I help?"

"Can you talk to her? I mean, if I can get her to agree?"

"Of course," I say. "But ethically, I can't talk to her without her parents' permission. I need a signed consent form. I appreciate your telling me about it, and I want to help."

I see her relief. "Doc, you taught me about what is safe and not safe in a relationship. I need to get her to understand that too."

I give her a few suggestions, and she nods.

Over the next few weeks, Julie calls me to say she's trying to set things up for Sarah to see me, and I am very relieved when Sarah's mother calls after three weeks and sets up a counseling appointment with me.

Sarah and her mother come in together to fill out the initial paperwork, then Sarah and I begin to talk alone.

"Before we start, I need to know something," Sarah blurts out. "Will you keep what I tell you just between us? Or will you tell other people about what we discuss?"

I'm straight with her. "I am required by law to report what you say under some specific conditions. One, if you tell me you are going to hurt yourself or someone else. Second, if you tell me about any child abuse, of yourself or anyone else."

She sighs deeply and then nods.

"Okay. So this all started with some of the mission trips I go on with the youth group at church."

She tells me that the previous summer she was so excited to be part of a mission trip to present Vacation Bible School to inner-city children who live in poverty. Sarah lights up as she talks about how much she loved working with the children and how attached she got to them during the week.

While the teens were preparing for the mission trip, the youth minister, Randall, seemed to focus on her and kept telling her that she had a gift for working with children. He spent time teaching Sarah about spiritual development and finding ways for Sarah to reach other children.

"I can look back and see that he was probably spending too much time with me," she says, "but at the time I was so excited about the mission, and he kept complimenting me and telling me how happy he was to be mentoring me."

After several months of preparation, the teens traveled nine hours for their mission trip. They spent a week eating unfamiliar local food, sleeping on the floor of the church, and taking showers at the inner-city outreach center. I see Sarah's eyes sparkle as she describes the adventure of third-world living.

But during the week they were on the mission trip, the youth minister continued to pull Sarah aside and talk with her about how the activities and presentations were going and make suggestions for the next day.

Sarah tells about the end of every day, when she would walk around the neighborhood with the youth minister as they talked. As they were walking on Thursday, the youth minister turned down an alley. Sarah walked with him and continued to talk about the day. Once they had walked far enough into the alley that other people couldn't easily see them, Randall stopped and turned to talk with Sarah.

He told Sarah that she was amazing. Sarah initially thought that the youth minister was talking about her work on the mission trip, but then he moved closer to Sarah and started kissing her.

"I was so surprised. I felt like I was frozen in place, but then I started kissing him back. I mean, I know I shouldn't have, but I really liked him, and . . . it felt good."

She looks at me, and I show her that I am listening, not judging.

"For a few minutes after the kissing part, he told me I was special, like sent by God to help him in his ministry. But then when we started walking back, he started talking about Vacation Bible School and acted like nothing had happened."

The following afternoon was their final day of the mission trip before starting the drive back home. Sarah says that she went on a walk with Randall that afternoon as well. They turned down the same alley again. He kissed Sarah again and also put his hands under her clothes and had Sarah rub his genital area.

Her head is down as she is telling me this. "I liked him, and I didn't want to get him in trouble, so I didn't tell anyone about it."

"What happened when you got home after the mission trip?"

"He was good at getting me alone, and I guess you could say we kept messing around. But not intercourse. I knew that was wrong."

"Anything else?"

Her head dips lower.

"Well, he keeps asking me to send him pictures of me. Like, without clothes." She looks up at me. "But I don't want to do that. And I don't want to get him in trouble, really. I just want this to go away. I feel smothered. I just want to hang out with my friends like before."

I spend some time explaining to Sarah that what her youth minister was doing was wrong and that it was also against the law. She is alarmed at this—crying, begging me not to tell anyone what he had done.

"He's an adult, Sarah. He is legally responsible for what he is doing. I know you're mature for your age, but legally you are a child." I begin to give her a list of sexual activities that are considered legally to be child abuse when they transpire between an adult and a minor. She nods as she agrees that many of those things had indeed happened.

"We can get through this," I assure her. "I know your mom is concerned. She needs to know about this. And this is something that will have to be reported to the police. Either I can report it, or you can. We can stop this."

Sarah looks stricken, but I see her back straighten. "I'll tell my mom," she says. "And I guess I'll tell the police too."

"We can get you through this," I tell her. And we will.

And who knows how many other vulnerable people would have been preyed on by this man if he hadn't been reported? If predators get away with their behaviors, they don't stop.

In order to help other parents know how to prevent a situation like this, I'd like you to look through the eyes of a predator.

A predator knows that we would not put our adolescent in the care of a stranger, and that we tend to trust people we know and who go to church with us. We have confidence in people we know—even though research shows us that kids are most frequently sexually abused by people we know and trust.

Of course, such a thing wouldn't happen on a mission trip, we tell ourselves. But on such outings, churches frequently have lower standards for volunteers, and trips often have a more lax structure than other church activities. The pedophile knows that, and just as parents will assume it's a safe situation, children will also feel relaxed and will let down their guard.

The predator seeks out situations in which church leaders and volunteers have had little or no training on how to identify warning signs of sexual abuse. He knows that if volunteers are not trained for the privilege of serving and protecting young people, he can operate more freely.

He doesn't want to undergo any criminal background checks that should be required for all staff and volunteers going on short-term mission trips; in fact, he's depending on you to feel embarrassed to ask him, even if you've only known him a short time. And although criminal background checks have become standard procedure for volunteers in children and youth ministries in U.S. churches, often mission trip volunteers aren't screened. (Remember that criminal background checks can never guarantee your volunteers are safe, since many sexual offenders have never been convicted. But such background checks do serve as a deterrent to those with prior convictions.)

A predator knows he can often fly under the radar when a youth group partners with other churches or missionary organizations to plan summer mission trips. He's depending on the parents not making the safety of their teen volunteers a priority, and he'll do all he can to distract you with schedules and a flurry of activities and fundraising. He doesn't want you to ask hard questions about the missionaries or organizations that your youth group partners with. He knows you don't want to be known as the picky, paranoid parent who digs into all the child protection policies—protection both for the kids in the youth group as well for as any kids at the mission's destination.

He knows it's a sacrifice of time and money to plan for such a trip—who has the time to undergo training?!

He knows that during mission trips, teens may be divided into multiple groups, making it more difficult to supervise teens and their interactions with others.

He knows that you think you're smart enough to spot a sexual offender by his appearance or mannerisms, and he's depending on your listening to the great things he says and does publicly and not watching how he behaves. One reason he can get away with what he does is because you and the other volunteers don't know about the grooming process. Offenders engage in a grooming process to gain the trust of potential victims. If there are people trained to recognize these behaviors, he probably won't want to operate under those conditions. He'll want to go somewhere people won't be on the lookout for grooming.

Grooming and Screening Behaviors

Here's the thing about grooming: At the beginning, it looks quite innocent. Sometimes people can participate in grooming behaviors unintentionally—but when you notice them, they should be red flags waving in front of your face. They should become the focus of someone's attention 24/7. The shift from innocent actions to predator behavior is demonstrated when someone begins to ignore the personal boundaries—whether physical, spiritual, or emotional—of someone else.

Stepping over physical boundaries can start small. You might watch someone roughhousing with kids and think, *He's just a big kid himself.* And that's what the predator wants to you to think. Then you won't think anything about the way he hugs, pushes hair away from their eyes, rubs their shoulders, tickles them, swats at them.

In these kinds of actions, the predator is consciously, deliberately screening you and your kids. Which kids will allow a progression of physical touches? Which parents will watch and not object in any way?

And from there, he's counting on you thinking he's sacrificial when he buys gifts and offers to give rides home to individual kids. He's depending on you to not speak up about when he talks about sex (after all, you're uncomfortable bringing that up with your kids, right?), and he is so cool when kids ask questions about sex.

Screening, screening, zeroing in on targets.

He knows you want your children to trust and lean on other Christian adults, to have good relationships with people of all ages. He knows that all effective leaders—especially those who deal with kids—have to be approachable and transparent. He knows we all are confident *we* can spot a fake a mile away.

But where a genuine leader will indeed allow himself or herself to be in many ways transparent, a predator will push limits on this. He will begin to treat a kid as an equal, an open book. He will appeal to the best part of your child, her noble helping heart, the heart of one who is going on a mission trip, a kid who wants to do something good for others. So the predator will position himself not only as someone who also wants to help others, but as someone who needs the comfort of the tender and trusting heart of a kid. He will begin making comments about his own secret hurts, knowing that teens want to help, to feel needed and trusted. He wants to create an emotional bond with kids, one in which the mentor/mentee relationship is blurred and secrets can be shared—and must be kept from others.

Here in the Southwestern United States, ranchers rely on a very valuable animal athlete known as a cutting horse. A man or woman on one of these highly trained horses can ride into a large group of cattle without causing a disturbance, and almost imperceptibly the horse and rider will select one specific cow or bull and begin to nudge that animal to the outside of the herd. Once at the perimeter, the horse's head is always focused on the head of the cow, matching it move for move, and expertly keeps that animal from returning to the group. If you've never seen one in action, a cutting horse's actions are a work of art.

So, also, are the actions of a predator to isolate individuals an art form. Unlike a cutting horse and its rider, who isolate an individual to give beneficial attention to an injury, for instance, the predator is isolating to harm, not to help. He will select one or more young people and convince each that he or she is "special"—in spirituality, in talents, in ability to understand "mature things"—and that this relationship must be kept from the knowledge of others to protect the leader.

Once exclusivity also becomes the goal of the young person, and there are secret gifts, conversations (spoken or in messages), and meetings, then more physical boundaries erode. The predator knows he can now achieve his goals. He can even make a kid think he or she has caused all this by being so necessary, so irresistible. And the child now has need and shame all tied up in a horrible emotional knot.

Strategies

Nip this in the bud. Every mission trip should have some simple rules for volunteers and teens that help adults recognize grooming behaviors.

- An adult should not be alone with teens or children. There should be a two-adult accountability procedure so that adult behavior can be monitored for the protection of both the student and the leader. This two-adult accountability mandates that no teen or child is alone with one adult for any reason. Infractions should be dealt with decisively, systematically, and uniformly so that all leaders understand this rule is nonnegotiable.
- All participants are required to travel in groups of at least three. The three-together rule should be understood by adults and teens alike.
- For sexual and physical safety, adults and teens need to stay within clearly outlined geographical boundaries of

the mission. Adults and teens should agree that they are expected to stay in well-lit and public areas when on the trip. In addition, they should understand that they need to stay in the assigned areas for housing, and they must sign an agreement concerning this and other behaviors on a mission trip.

- At least two adults should be in a room with teens or children. Having only one adult in a room provides access for abuse or an opportunity for an accusation that could destroy the adult sponsor. The adults should not sleep in the same beds as children unless the children are their own.
- Volunteers should complete training about the difference between appropriate and inappropriate touch.
- Kids sometimes abuse other kids. Volunteers must be on the lookout for this.

Another Sad Scenario from the News

Matthew Durham from Oklahoma traveled to Kenya in 2014 to serve as a summer missionary in a Nairobi orphanage, working at the Upendo Children's Home with neglected children. He'd previously volunteered there three times, and no suspicion arose when he requested to stay at an "overflow bunk" in the school rather than at off-site facilities with sponsor families.

A school caretaker noticed that Durham was lying beside some of the children on their beds at night and hugging them frequently. After investigations, Matthew was convicted of sexual assaults against three girls and a boy, and sentenced to forty years in prison.

While following the guidelines in this chapter won't guarantee that everyone will be safe, it will encourage predators to find a different location to target children and teens, and as more people follow these guidelines, it will make it more difficult for them to succeed.

But they're predators. They'll keep searching for prey; that's their nature. A good way to illustrate and discuss this is to research with your child some of the species in nature that try to look like something harmless so they can catch their prey, like a flower mantis—a vicious insect that looks like a delicate flower.

Jesus talked about the same kind of thing when He told people to watch out for false prophets in disguise (Matthew 7:15), and that's how the phrase "wolf in sheep's clothing" came into our vocabulary.

The predator you'd never suspect? That's as new as tomorrow's headlines and as old as the Bible itself.

Messages for Your Teen

Keep nurturing that warrior heart. Kids can learn to safeguard themselves if you give them the tools. Keep them safe by giving them the information and support they need to make good decisions. Your teens should know about God's plan for sexuality in marriage and recognize sexual behaviors.

- Teens should know what sexual and emotional limits are healthy in a relationship and how to tell other people about those limits.
- If someone has violated the emotional or sexual limits your teens set, your teenagers should recognize that it is dangerous and speak up immediately.
- Let your teens know that they have the right at any point to say no to a sexual behavior.

- Teach your children safety skills for group gatherings. Teach them to pour their own beverage and keep it in their sight. Help them recognize that it is easy for anyone to slip drugs or alcohol into their beverages.
- Teach your teenagers to be aware of where they are hanging out and to avoid places that keep them isolated from others. Teens may feel like they can take care of themselves, but they don't have the life experiences to recognize when they are in danger.
- Help your teens learn to trust their instincts. If they feel that a person or situation is not safe, they should leave immediately.
- Help your teens recognize that they need a back-up plan no matter where they go. This plan should include telling someone they trust where they are going. They should always have a person to call who will come immediately to get them.
- Teach your teens that technology can open the door to predators and allow them access to personal information.

Warning Signs of Abuse

The abused teen may

- have nightmares and/or images in their head about the assault;
- exhibit changes in eating patterns and experience weight gain or loss;
- have bruising or physical injuries;
- show changes in school performance or behavior;

- pay less attention to hygiene, appearance, or clothing style;
- show signs of depression, lack of energy, or changes in sleep;
- drink or use drugs; and
- engage in self-harm behaviors or have suicidal thoughts.

➡ WHAT YOU SHOULD DO

If you suspect your teen has been sexually or physically abused, remember not to overreact emotionally in front of your child. Let the child know you want to keep him or her safe—that it's your job, and you want to do it.

Take your concerns to a doctor, a social worker, or the police. You don't have to know that your child is not safe, you just have to suspect it to seek out professional assistance. And of course, don't leave your teen with any person they fear.

16

Abuse by Family/Trusted Friend
The Coach

My first meeting two weeks ago with Carol and Paul left me with the impression that these were two very nice people who were at the end of their rope. Their normally sociable sixteen-year-old daughter, Jenny, the oldest of three girls, has begun making strange and unreasonable demands.

Jenny wanted to change schools, even though she's starting her sophomore year of high school and had been an outstanding basketball player as a freshman. But now she doesn't play with the heart she once did. No drive. Just going through the drills and the motions. And Carol had fielded some calls from two teachers who said that this semester Jenny seemed distracted and sometimes almost rude. Jenny's grades were suffering, and nobody could seem to make her care.

She didn't want to hang out with her teammates as she did before, and even though she kept going to church, she sat on the edge of the group during Bible class and didn't go to any of the youth activities. Not even planning the summer vacation with some family friends—a trip to the Grand Canyon—seemed to interest her as it once had. In fact, she talked of attending a summer science camp scheduled for the same time as the vacation. Her reasons were vague and she never named names, so Paul and Carol wondered if there was some bullying going on, or something else. Maybe someone had broken her heart. Maybe Jenny would tell a counselor.

When Jenny did talk to me earlier today, I told her over and over that I have seen how much her parents love her, and that they will help her through this. She eventually talked to me about why she had changed.

Now Jenny is waiting in another room as I tell Paul and Carol that they are about to have a very difficult time when Jenny comes into the room to tell her parents something. Tears come into their eyes.

"It's important that you be very aware of how you are reacting when she tells you," I tell them. "You will probably be angry, and that's natural. You may feel guilty. But as you listen, be prepared first to say how much you love her. She is the one who has had to hold this inside for so long. Be sure to hug her and let her know that.

"You have an awesome daughter," I tell them. "She is being very brave. I offered to tell you, but she wanted to do it herself."

When I bring Jenny into the room, I seat her between her parents on the long couch. She gathers herself together, hugging herself at first. I catch her eye, nod at her, and jump-start the conversation.

"Jenny, your parents know that there is something difficult you want to tell them. I haven't told them anything about what you want to share, but they love you and they are here because they want to support you."

My heart is hurting. My stomach roils.

I am so proud of what Carol does next. She takes her daughter's hand between her own, sheltering, warming.

"Honey, we love you and we won't be disappointed in you. You can talk to us. We will figure all of this out."

Paul's eyes are wet. He reaches toward Jenny, patting her on the shoulder. She begins to sob, and it is minutes before she can talk again.

"Do you remember when Coach Jackson took the basketball team to Houston to play in that tournament last year?"

"I remember," says Carol, and I make a mental note that Carol once mentioned Coach Clara Jackson and her husband. The couple were their good friends, and the two families were even planning to visit the Grand Canyon together.

The story comes out. The trusted friend and coach, who told the teenage athletes that the tournament hotels didn't have enough beds, had molested Jenny in the hotel bed they shared. It continued the next night, but in daylight hours the coach acted as if nothing had happened.

"Stuff like that happened a lot after that trip," says Jenny. "Coach would give me rides and do stuff. She would wait until the other players left practice and then it would start again. I didn't want to tell anybody what Coach Jackson was doing because I knew she would get in trouble. That's why I wanted to change schools this year."

Paul gets up now. He takes Jenny's hands and pulls her up from the couch and wraps his arms around her.

"I love you," he says firmly. "I am not disappointed in you." But then his voice breaks. "I'm so sorry I didn't keep you safe."

Carol stands up, trying to envelop them both in her arms.

I allow them time to hold each other. Jenny yields to them, but she is stronger already. For her, the worst part is over. The burden she has been carrying for months is now shared with those who love her, who will help her carry it. She is ready to sit back down on the couch and take the next step.

That next step is to talk to a police detective, who assures Jenny that she has done the right thing and outlines what will follow: A grand jury will decide whether to indict Coach Jackson; most likely the coach will be suspended during the investigation, to keep other kids safe. The detective assures Jenny and her family that she won't have to have any contact with the coach, and that there is victims assistance available. Victims assistance programs help meet victims' physical and psychological needs and help victims navigate the justice system so they are not re-victimized as a perpetrator is prosecuted.

After he leaves, I have important instructions for Paul and Carol: "You are going to feel confused and troubled about this. That's natural, a sign of your concern for Jenny. You will have a lot of questions too. But you need to share them with me, not with Jenny. You have a very important role to help Jenny, to help her feel safe in her own home. She shouldn't have to feel anxious that you will try to ask her more questions about this. She doesn't need to relive this anymore."

I make eye contact with Jenny and hold it. "Jenny, you make the decision if you want to talk about this further. It's your choice, and yours alone, if you want to talk to your parents. I can see that they love you very much."

Paul and Carol nod.

Before they leave, Carol has a question.

"What about testifying? Will Jenny have to go to court too?"

"A lot of people think from TV that victims have to confront their accusers, but that almost never is necessary for a juvenile victim," I reassure them. "In fact, it will probably never make it to a courtroom."

(I know from my experience that most juvenile sexual assault cases don't require victims to testify in court because usually the perpetrator either accepts a plea agreement or there is digital evidence that supports the victim's story. It still amazes me how many perpetrators send inappropriate text messages or videotape their sexual interactions with their victims.)

In the end, it was courageous, unwavering, united support from Paul and Carol that got them through this situation. Coach Jackson was charged with sexual assault. Because Jackson was both a teacher and a coach of many students at the school, and the identity of the victim of the crime was never made public, Jenny's privacy was protected.

She stayed at the school she loved, had the best basketball season of her high school career, and through counseling strengthened the kind of warrior heart that helped her triumph in many situations in her later life.

Sports and Abuse

Paul and Carol, like most parents, might wonder if this happened because their daughter has been caught up in this twenty-first-century world where sex is visible everywhere and teenagers seem to be more sexually active. But they would be wrong; the CDC says, "Longer-term trends, from 1988 to 2011–2015, show declines in the percentage of teenagers who were sexually experienced." That means that teenagers today are *less likely* to be engaging voluntarily in sexual behavior than they were twenty years ago when Paul and Carol were dating.[1]

Perhaps, a parent might reason, it's because of a culture where sexual behavior and gender issues are in the headlines. They might wonder if easy access to porn causes people to be sexual offenders. But I'd have to tell anyone with that impression that my own years of practice, and all the research to which I have access, don't show such a cause-and-effect connection from those two factors. A thorough analysis of the relationship between pornography and sexual abuse found that there is no causal relationship between pornography and sexual abuse. While viewing pornography may be a contributing factor to sexual abuse, there are many men and women who view pornography who never engage in sexually assaultive behavior.[2]

If they're like most parents, at first they may not be able to reconcile the mental image of their trusted friend with the person who has hurt their child. *Who could do such a thing? It isn't a stranger—it's a friend!* They feel betrayal—profound, bitter, inescapable.

Children participating in sports are particularly vulnerable to sexual abuse: Research indicates 40 to 50 percent of athletes have experienced it, ranging from mild harassment to severe abuse. If the coaches are affiliated with a public or private school, they may have undergone a screening process and a criminal background check. However, not all states or schools require a screening process and criminal background check. Many coaches are not affiliated with private and public schools and may work independently or for gyms or clubs. In these situations, it is unlikely that the coaches have undergone any screening or a criminal background check.

While we give coaches great access to our children, we frequently do not consider whether the coaches are safe or unsafe. In some cases, normal boundaries that exist with non-family members can gradually disappear into an intimate coach relationship.

Sometimes the coaching relationship evolves into a surrogate parent relationship. The coach becomes as trusted or more trusted than the athlete's parents because the athlete spends so much time with the coach, and the coach has so much power over the athlete's success in competition.

This power and influence means coaches can control the opportunities available to athletes. In addition, coaches and athletes are often in close physical proximity. In many sports, it's common for coaches to touch athletes to help them improve how they use their bodies in performance.

Some inherent factors in the coach-athlete relationship make athletes particularly vulnerable to being abused. First, there is a clear imbalance in the power between athletes and coaches. Athletic competition is a hierarchical system with performance-based awards, which can lead to athletes being very compliant with coaches who can give them what they see as advantages or rewards.

Second, athletes frequently have intense peer competition and jealousy, which can lead to isolation from peers. Further, the coach-athlete relationship can provide a separation of the athlete from not only peers, but family and other mentors.

Many athletes travel to competitions; this is part of the culture of adolescent sports. As parents, we don't question our children traveling with their team or with coaches or sponsors. Yet sexual abuse is more than twice as likely to happen on team trips.

Why is this? Traveling for competition frequently involves mixed sexes and ages traveling together, with coaches making decisions on how adults and athletes will share rooms. Sometimes adult leaders and coaches naïvely make these decisions based on what is the least expensive option, rather than first considering safety. In many situations, there is a lack of oversight and supervision during travel—especially on buses. A lot of bullying and abuse can happen in the back seats.

Surprisingly, research shows that the location of an event is also a risk factor. For instance, national and international competitions and tournaments, and travel situations in which an adolescent is alone in a car with the coach, are higher risk. Even the "character" of the sport or league can set up an abuse situation—those

185

that focus more on performance than on athletes' well-being can increase risk. For example, some coaches or leagues will allow an injured player to risk long-term disability simply because they want to win the game. When a player's well-being is secondary to achievement, there is an increased risk of abuse.

There are "red flag" behaviors that, though they do not always indicate abuse, certainly do indicate inappropriate boundaries between coaches and athletes. These behaviors include when the coach

- tries to be alone with the athlete, sometimes spending one-on-one time in private practice sessions;
- singles out one athlete for special attention, or spends more time with one athlete than with the others;
- gives gifts to just one athlete;
- touches athletes in ways not related to training for the sport or seems overly physical, beyond what is necessary for handling and teaching. (Full-body hugs are not necessary. Hugging from the side and high-fives can suffice.);
- asks the athlete not to talk about their personal encounters;
- spends a lot of time in the locker room;
- has long phone calls, sends frequent emails, or engages in frequent texting with an athlete;
- tells athletes sexual or inappropriate jokes and stories;
- comments on an athlete's appearance with remarks that are not related to the sport;
- makes it difficult for parents to attend competitions away from home and/or transports one athlete to practices or athletic events alone; or

- holds team sleepovers and/or lock-ins that provide an opportunity to continue the abusive relationship even if the whole team is invited.

Signs of Abuse

In addition to watching the interaction between coaches and your adolescent, be aware of how your teen's behavior may change if he or she is being sexually abused by a coach. Such behavior changes may be evident when your child

- is no longer interested in the sport or starts missing practices;
- begins performing significantly below his or her abilities;
- tries to avoid a particular coach or location;
- begins to struggle with illness;
- engages in overly sexualized behavior that is not appropriate for his or her age or situation;
- suddenly has eating or sleeping issues;
- is irritable and angry when they have not demonstrated these emotions previously;
- develops new concerns about being dirty and wants to wash often;
- is no longer interested in school, or his or her grades drop; or
- is suddenly sad, withdrawn, or isolated.

Preventing Sexual Abuse

Insist on screenings: In any situation where your child is in the care of other adults, those adults must undergo a screening process and pass a criminal background check. If the school or organization the coaches work for or with does not perform screening and background checks, you should ask the coach to let you conduct your own background check. Background checks can easily be completed online with minimal cost.

If a coach or coaches won't agree to the background check, find another coach. No amount of athletic achievement is worth putting your child at risk.

Physicians and Trainers

The recent court cases involving Dr. Nassar and the years of alleged abuse of gymnasts shows what can happen when team trainers and physicians have unrestricted access to your children. When you take your child to your family and/or team physician, there must always be at least one additional person in the room with the doctor during the examination. Generally, a parent should be in the room and should position him or herself to be able to see the physician's hands at all times. Notice if the medical professional places his or her genitals or breasts near your child or rubs against them in any way that makes you or your child uncomfortable. If you leave the room, a nurse or other medical assistant should enter the room.

If you don't think your children are getting the treatment they need, get a second opinion. If your children don't want to see a trainer or team physician, try to ask a few low-key questions to see if you can uncover why. Even if you can't figure out why your children don't like a trainer or medical provider, insist that they see a different medical professional.

Teach your adolescents how to protect themselves using the information provided in the "What They Should Know" section for this age group. Inoculate them against predators by having loving, protective relationships with your children.

The Role of Self-Esteem

Praise your children for their efforts in their sports performances, and find ways to congratulate them on their successes. Children with low self-esteem are targets. You can fill that gap in their hearts.

Most parents explain to their children that there are dangers to them out in the world, but they should learn that a coach can also hurt them. While coaches tend to be put on a pedestal, it is important to remind your children that their value does not come from the approval of a coach or from athletic achievement; rather, their value comes from being a child of God.

Sports are the best example of success with a built-in shelf life. Even top professional athletes find that age, injury, and other factors will not allow them to compete with younger talented athletes. Your kid may not be able to see that end of the process, just the immediate glamor of the roar of the crowd, the championship trophy, the possibility of scholarships.

What's truly valuable? It's not the thing itself, but the person who pays for and treasures something that sets the value. Jesus chose the lowliest and least brawny of all animals—a sparrow—to make a point about where true worth comes from. (You've never heard of a sparrow race, right? and nobody is breeding sparrows for profit.) But Jesus said, "Are not two sparrows sold for a penny? Yet not one of them will fall to the ground outside your Father's care. And even the very hairs of your head are all numbered. So don't be afraid; you are worth more than many sparrows" (Matthew 10:29–31).

Go outside. Point out a sparrow or other little bird to your son or daughter and talk about how the God of the universe, with all His responsibilities, is acutely aware of and concerned about plain, unremarkable, nameless little birds.

He doesn't wait for them to prove themselves on an athletic field or win a race. He knows every feather. He cares about them.

Tell your child God loves and cares deeply for him or her. And then follow up with words and actions that show your children how much you love them too, no matter whether they win or lose.

Messages for Your Teen

Keep nurturing that warrior heart. Kids can learn to safeguard themselves if you give them the tools. Keep them safe by giving them the information and support they need to make good decisions. Your teens should know about God's plan for sexuality in marriage and recognize sexual behaviors.

- Teens should know what sexual and emotional limits are healthy in a relationship and how to tell other people about those limits.
- Teenagers should recognize that it is dangerous if someone violates the emotional or sexual limits they have set, and speak up immediately.
- Let your teens know that they have the right at any point to say no to a sexual behavior.
- Teach your children safety skills for group gatherings. Teach them to pour their own beverage and keep it in their sight. Help them recognize that it is easy for anyone to slip drugs or alcohol into their beverages.

- Teach your teenagers to be aware of where they are hanging out and to avoid places that keep them isolated from others. Teens may feel like they can take care of themselves, but they don't have the life experiences to recognize when they are in danger.
- Help your teens learn to trust their instincts. If they feel that a person or situation is not safe, they should leave immediately.
- Help your teens recognize that they need a back-up plan no matter where they go. This plan should include telling someone they trust where they are going. They should always have a person to call who will come immediately to get them.
- Teach your teens that technology can open the door to predators and allow them access to personal information.

Warning Signs of Abuse

The abused teen may
- have nightmares and/or images about the assault in their head;
- exhibit changes in eating patterns and experience weight gain or loss;
- have bruising or physical injuries;
- show changes in school performance or behavior;
- pay less attention to hygiene, appearance, or clothing style;
- show signs of depression, lack of energy, changes in sleep;
- drink or use drugs; or
- engage in self-harm behaviors or have suicidal thoughts.

→ *WHAT YOU SHOULD DO*

If you suspect your teen has been sexually or physically abused, remember not to overreact emotionally in front of your child. Let your child know you want to keep him or her safe—that it's your job, and you want to do it.

Take your concerns to a doctor, a social worker, or the police. You don't have to know that your child is not safe, you just have to suspect it to seek out professional assistance. And of course, don't leave your teen with any person they fear.

17

Abuse by Peer

Dating Violence

One of my former students, Barbara, is a counselor at a private high school, and she called to tell me of her concerns over one of her students named Debbie. Debbie's parents told my colleague that Debbie had been texting sexually suggestive information to her boyfriend, Aaron.

As her parents monitored her phone, they discovered that Debbie and Aaron had been going to his parents' house during lunch, so they grounded Debbie—no use of her phone or car for a month.

At the end of the month when Debbie got phone privileges again, her parents turned on the GPS monitor so they could track where she went. For the first two weeks, she was restricted to eating lunch on campus, and the phone indicated what Barbara confirmed: Debbie was staying at school. The relationship between Debbie and Aaron seemed to weather all these changes even when her parents eased the restrictions and said Debbie could now go off campus with her friends—again, confirmed by the phone's GPS.

But Debbie's parents and Barbara noticed some alarming changes in Debbie. Though she had seemed withdrawn before, now she seemed to be losing interest in school and she kept to herself more than ever.

That's when Barbara and Debbie's parents set up an appointment for Debbie with me. After I discussed the counseling relationship and we filled out paperwork, they agreed I should meet with Debbie alone while they waited in the lobby.

As Debbie sits before me, I see just what they were talking about.

She won't make eye contact with me. She is huddled in a corner of the couch, almost as if she is willing it to enfold her. Her knees are pulled up to her chest.

"Do you want to talk to me?" I ask. Her nod is almost imperceptible. But I see her struggle to begin.

"Hey, I like card games. Do you? Want to play a hand or two with me?" After a few minutes, I see her shoulders relaxing.

I begin to ask her a few questions while we play cards. To my surprise, Debbie begins by telling me she was actually relieved when her parents found out that she had been going to Aaron's house at lunch.

"Why was that a relief?"

Her shoulders come back up. She swallows.

"He—Aaron—made me go to his parents' house."

"How did he make you go?"

At first, she doesn't answer. We play cards in silence for a few minutes.

She looks down. "He hurts me if I don't do what he says."

"How? In what way does he hurt you?"

Her voice is so quiet I have to lean forward to hear her.

"He slaps me. And he chokes me."

We talk about how Debbie has the right to say no to her boyfriend and how her boyfriend doesn't own her. She nods. But when

I ask her what else he makes her do when she goes with him, she won't meet my eyes again.

"He makes me have sex with him too, and send him pictures of me on my phone."

A little at a time, Debbie describes how her boyfriend would slap her until she would undress at his house. Other times he would hit and kick her in the stomach when she didn't do what he told her to do.

"How recently has this happened?"

She shrugs. "Day before yesterday." She looks up. "But it was my fault this time. I wasn't . . . good enough." She touches her stomach, seemingly unaware as she does so.

I tip my head and then motion to her waist. Slowly, she lifts her shirt and I tell myself not to gasp at the mottled purple and green and yellow on her abdomen: old bruises and new.

Wait, I think to myself. She's going to lunch with her friends, right? And her parents are keeping a close eye on her when she's not at school, right? When is this happening?

"When? How can he get away with doing this at school?" I ask.

"Oh, he makes me give my phone to one of my friends and she takes it to lunch with her. I go with Aaron, like, every school day."

The story comes out. During lunch, her boyfriend sexually and physically assaults her at his parents' house. When they get back to school, Debbie meets her friends in the parking lot, retrieves her cell phone, and walks into the school building with her friends. The phone's GPS doesn't lie. But it also doesn't show where Debbie was.

We continue to play cards. Little by little, Debbie tells me she doesn't even like Aaron, but she doesn't know how to make him stop. And she's afraid to tell her parents because she believes they'll be angry about the sex, the deception.

"I'm afraid they'll pull me out of school, away from my friends," she says.

We talk about how important it is for Debbie to feel safe. And I reassure her that her parents love her and want her to be safe.

"You know you're not to blame for being afraid, don't you?" I see her barely move her head in assent. "And that what Aaron is doing is against the law?"

I expect her to resist the idea of involving the police, but she seems relieved.

"And your parents have to know. Would you like for me to tell them?"

She wants to tell them herself. When they come into the room, they listen, but right away they put their arms around her and tell her they love her. And that they want her to be safe.

By the end of the day, the police are involved and her parents get a restraining order to keep Debbie's boyfriend away from her. They notify the school about the restraining order, and Aaron is suspended during the investigation.

Eventually, Debbie's boyfriend takes a plea agreement that results in him being on probation and having to attend counseling to address his violence. He is not allowed to enroll in Debbie's school again.

Debbie, for her part, does very well in her counseling sessions and is looking forward to a new school year and new relationships. Her heart will continue to heal, but it will be a protective heart. A warrior heart not only survives this sort of thing, but will help her peers avoid it too.

Teen Dating Violence

Almost 1 in 10 teenagers reported being hit, slapped, or physically hurt on purpose by their boyfriend or girlfriend in the last year.[1] Approximately 1 in 5 women and nearly 1 in 7 men who experience rape, physical violence, or stalking first experienced some form of dating violence quite young: between eleven and seventeen years of age.[2] Teen dating violence includes physical, sexual, or emotional violence as well as stalking between a current or former dating partner.

Violence in teen dating relationships is as prevalent, harmful, and dangerous as it is in adult domestic-violence cases. In violent teen relationships, perpetrators exert power and control over their victims. But teens typically use different methods than adults to control their victims. Teens maximize social media like Facebook, Twitter, and Snapchat to influence and control their victims. The perpetrators use technology to track and stalk victims. In addition, perpetrators frequently demand their victims engage in sexually suggestive activities through email or social media.

How prevalent is this? *More than 1 in 3 teenagers have sent or posted sexually suggestive emails or text messages, and teens are frequently coerced by an intimate partner.*

Teens often filter information differently from adults. For example, teens may not assess a relationship as "abusive" if they don't consider the relationship to be serious. Teens may believe that abuse only occurs in long-term, intimate relationships, and may not recognize that they are experiencing abuse. Even worse, teens may interpret violence as an act of love. Research shows that 25 to 46 percent of female adolescents involved in violent relationships interpreted the violence as an act of love.[3]

However, adolescent perpetrators are also likely to use non-physical abuse, such as threats, peer pressure, economic manipulation, and/or verbal harassment. Teen dating violence can take many forms. Sometimes it ends in rape or murder. Short of that, abusers shove, grab, punch, choke, slap, pinch, and wrench limbs. They threaten, criticize, intimidate, and stalk. Often they justify this as jealousy motivated by "love."

Generally, teen dating violence involves a pattern of abusive behaviors that cause fear and harm. But if one incident is observed, it is likely that it is a pattern of behavior rather than an isolated incident.

Teen dating violence hurts the emotional development of teens. Abusive, unhealthy, and violent relationships can have both short-term and long-term effects on teens. Youth who experience dating violence are more likely to experience depression, anxiety, eating disorders, poor school performance, and drug and alcohol use. Teen dating violence also impacts lifetime earnings and relationships.[4]

Most teens who are coerced into sexual intercourse are fifteen or younger when they are victimized for the first time. When females are victimized between the ages of fifteen and twenty years of age, more than 1 in 4 report that their partners were actively trying to get them pregnant.[5]

When victims try to cut ties and leave their abuser, their perpetrators may use technology and engage in stalking their victims. Stalking is a real danger to teen victims, and in 20 percent of teen stalking cases, a weapon is used by the abuser.[6]

Teen dating violence is the leading cause of death for African American girls ages fifteen to nineteen, and it is the second leading cause of death for adolescent girls of other races.[7] And it's not always the abuser who ends the life: When teens can't cope with dating violence, some will end their own lives.[8]

Reasons for Teen Violence

We can't afford not to address this with our children. We have to talk to them about what is a healthy dating relationship and what's not. While our silence about it can contribute to our children getting involved in an abusive relationship, our culture makes kids fight an uphill battle already in learning about dating relationships. Peers, adults, and celebrity "role models" too frequently include violence in relationships.

Let's turn the spotlight on ourselves as parents, first. We may not even recognize that we have unhealthy patterns in our own relationships. Kids watch our relationships and draw conclusions, and when we allow—or practice—verbal or emotional abuse in a relationship, teens may see this and recognize the little value we may place on our partners. Then, if their friends are involved in dating violence, they accept that violence in a teen relationship is acceptable too.

Talking to Our Teens

Teens often don't recognize that they are in a violent relationship because we don't talk with them about violent relationships. One way of introducing the subject is by pointing to examples of healthy and unhealthy behaviors in the media and in family history (almost everyone has that kind of skeleton in their family tree's closet). Telling stories is great. But here's where listening is so important. We can't just lecture. Let them talk about it, react, speculate. As best you can, don't interrupt.

When our teens don't want to talk, step back and let them know we are available when they are ready to talk, and that we will be supportive and nonjudgmental because we are the ones who have opened the door for discussion. When they do broach the subject and ask questions, if you don't know the answer to a question, admit you don't know. As in so many areas of life, admitting what we don't know gains us credibility with our kids.

Sometimes when we're protective of our kids, we forget to tell them that dating should be fun and not stressful. But along with that, we remind them that they have warrior hearts, and that they have a right to say no—and so do the people they date.

The Holy Spirit guides believers of all ages. Let your children know that if a relationship feels uncomfortable or frightening in any way, they should listen to those protective warning promptings from Him. And you are also there to listen. As a general rule, *any* relationship that scares them or makes them uncomfortable is one that you can help with—it should be supervised by adults, and probably needs to be ended.

If you need some ideas for how to start a conversation with your teens, here are some openings:

- Are any of your friends dating?
- What are their relationships like?
- What would you want in a relationship?
- What do you consider to be red flags for a dating relationship that's not healthy?
- Do you know what you would do if you witnessed or experienced abuse?
- Has anyone you know posted bad stuff about a friend online? Why would they do this?
- How would you feel if someone you were dating texted you all day to ask you what you're doing and where you're going?

The Truth about the Future

Tell kids that they can't wait around for a violent boyfriend or girlfriend to "get better."

Move on! A warrior heart knows it should not fight every battle.

Girls especially are prone to be attracted to "bad boys." Discuss with your children that is not their job to "fix" or redeem other people. There are mission fields of all sorts that are great places for teenagers to get involved, but they can't take on the responsibilities that even professionals are cautious in dealing with.

A violent or possessive boyfriend or girlfriend will almost certainly be a violent or possessive spouse.

It's a hard fact: Teenagers who are violent often continue to be violent in adulthood and become perpetrators of domestic violence. The sad other side of that coin is that similarly, teen victims of violence may accept abusive behavior as normal and thus continue to be involved in violent relationships in adulthood.

Once a teen recognizes that he or she is a victim in an abusive relationship, they may not want to admit it. They may fear punishment if it comes to light that they were under the influence of drugs or alcohol when the abuse occurred, for example. Or they might be embarrassed. A teen may reason that the physical danger can get worse if they reveal the violence in the relationship. And they would be right to think this: Based on research with adults, escalated violence when a victim leaves the relationship is a real concern and issue.

Here's another grim reality: sex trafficking. In the next chapter, we will look at sex trafficking in a kidnapping situation. But it also happens with partners that teens know—not just with strangers. In the teen dating context, it is a serious form of intimate partner violence in which a batterer forces his victim into prostitution as part of his abuse. Girls who have been subjected to sexual abuse are particularly likely targets of traffickers, so there are often many layers and instances of trauma.

How can we protect our kids from such violence? One way is by modeling in our own families the ideal of protecting those we love, so that your child understands that self-sacrifice is the basis of love, not self-pleasing at the expense of another. Dating and marriage have no place for violence. In Ephesians chapter 5, after introducing the idea that Christians should submit to one another in love, Paul tells fathers how to protect. Even though some families do not have fathers, the ideals and the principles that connect love to sacrifice still hold true.

> Husbands, love your wives, just as Christ loved the church and gave himself up for her to make her holy, cleansing her by the washing with water through the word, and to present her to himself as a radiant church, without stain or wrinkle or any other blemish, but holy and blameless. *In this same way, husbands ought to love their wives as their own bodies. He who loves his wife loves himself. After all, no one ever hated their own body, but they feed and care for their body, just as Christ does the church—for we are members of his body.*
>
> Ephesians 5:25–30, italics added

Even if your own marriage doesn't yet exemplify this, it's the dream relationship for your child, the end goal of dating and love for those who marry.

Messages for Your Teen

Keep nurturing that warrior heart. Kids can learn to safeguard themselves if you give them the tools. Keep them safe by giving them the information and support they need to make good decisions. Your teens should know about God's plan for sexuality in marriage and recognize sexual behaviors.

- Teens should know what sexual and emotional limits are healthy in a relationship and how to tell other people about those limits.

- Teenagers should recognize that it is dangerous if someone violates the emotional or sexual limits they have set and speak up immediately.
- Let your teens know that they have the right at any point to say no to a sexual behavior.
- Teach your children safety skills for group gatherings. Teach them to pour their own beverage and keep it in their sight. Help them recognize that it is easy for anyone to slip drugs or alcohol into their beverages.
- Teach your teenagers to be aware of where they are hanging out and to avoid places that keep them isolated from others. Teens may feel like they can take care of themselves, but they don't have the life experiences to recognize when they are in danger.
- Help your teens learn to trust their instincts. If they feel that a person or situation is not safe, they should leave immediately.
- Help your teens recognize that they need a back-up plan no matter where they go. This plan should include telling someone they trust where they are going. They should always have a person to call who will come immediately to get them.
- Teach your teens that technology can open the door to predators and allow them access to personal information.

Warning Signs of Abuse

The abused teen may

- have nightmares and/or images in their head about the assault;

- exhibit changes in eating patterns and experience weight gain or loss;
- have bruising or physical injuries;
- show changes in school performance or behavior;
- pay less attention to hygiene, appearance, or clothing style;
- show signs of depression, lack of energy, or changes in sleep;
- drink or use drugs; or
- engage in self-harm behaviors or have suicidal thoughts.

➡ WHAT YOU SHOULD DO

If you suspect your teen has been sexually or physically abused, remember not to overreact emotionally in front of your child. Let your child know you want to keep him or her safe—that it's your job, and you want to do it.

Take your concerns to a doctor, a social worker, or the police. You don't have to know that your child is not safe, you just have to suspect it to seek out professional assistance. And of course, don't leave your teen with any person they fear.

18

Abuse by Strangers

Malls and Other Public Places

Celia was referred to me by the victims assistance agency in another part of the state. She had been a victim of abduction, and her parents had relocated to a small town to help protect her, thinking they could keep a closer eye on her. Celia was not typical of teens who are abducted and become part of sex trafficking, because she was abducted by a stranger. Over ninety percent of victims are introduced into sex trafficking by someone they know.

When Celia first came to my office, she just wanted to vent. It was stupid to have to move to the middle of nowhere, to leave her school and her friends, she told me. And nobody asked her, they just did it. Her whole ample body was shaking with anger.

"Why do your parents say they moved?" I asked her.

"I guess because of what happened to me," she said. "They keep talking about a 'fresh start' where nobody knows me. As if that would change what already happened."

After several weeks of counseling, Celia was able to process reasons why her parents had moved the family. Her parents attended some of the sessions, and I refereed so they could verbalize their reasons for the move. As Celia calmed, we reached a point where we could talk about the abduction itself.

As she begins to tell me about the day her young life changed forever, I ache with sympathy for her. I already know this story, but I want there to be another ending to it, a rewind and do-over.

"I was at the mall with two of my friends," Celia begins. "We all go to the same middle school. Nobody was really shopping, we were just hanging out and having fun. Our parents let us go together and dropped us off, and it felt like they were finally beginning to realize we weren't babies anymore, that we could do things like other teenagers at school talked about."

"You didn't feel in danger?"

"Not at all! We weren't doing anything wrong. We were looking at clothes, and then this really beautiful girl comes up and asked my opinion about a dress she was thinking about buying. I couldn't believe she wanted my opinion—the clothes she was wearing were fabulous and she looked like she was in high school. And there she was, saying she liked my style!"

Flattered, Celia was happy to help the older girl shop. When the older girl, Maggie, could not find what she wanted in the store, she asked Celia if she would help her look in another store. Celia talked to her friends and they agreed to go to the next store. Celia felt important because the older girl was listening to her recommendations and seemed to like her. After looking in three different stores, Maggie found some clothes she wanted to buy.

"But then she reached in her purse," Celia continues, "and found out she'd left her wallet in her car. We decided my friends would stay with her stuff and I'd walk her out to her car to get it."

At this point Celia looks down and her voice becomes like a recording, telling a story. "There was a small sports car parked next to a van. Maggie walked up to the driver's side of the car and kept looking around in her purse for keys while I waited—but then all of a sudden a man walked up behind me and told me to get in the van."

To Celia's surprise, Maggie unlocked the van door and the man showed Celia a gun. Celia was so startled that she got in. There, the man tied her arms and legs with zip ties and put duct tape on her mouth.

Celia's face flushes red. "I even heard Maggie telling the guy how easy it had been to get me to come to the car with her. I started to cry, because I knew I was really in trouble."

Back in the store, Celia's friends became concerned when Celia didn't return. They called their parents, who called Celia's parents. The mall security and local police were notified, and although video footage showed the two girls leaving the mall, unfortunately there were no cameras monitoring the parking lot where the van was parked.

An Amber Alert was issued. After two weeks, a convenience-store clerk recognized Celia and quietly called the police when she came into the store with her abductor. Celia was rescued and returned to her parents.

Rescued. But not restored. Celia has only hazy memories and thinks that she was drugged during most of the two weeks. To this day, she continues to have nightmares even though she has little recall of what happened. In her nightmares, she is being sexually assaulted. Indeed, when she was examined, tests showed she had been both drugged and raped.

Celia has a difficult road ahead of her, but she has supportive parents and peers. I see her responding well to counseling and have great hopes for her future.

About Abductions

Teenagers are the most frequent victims of both non-family abductions and stereotypical kidnappings—81 percent were children twelve or older.[1] In non-family abductions, the abductors do not intend to ask for a ransom or return the child to the family; rather, the teens are generally sold into sex trafficking or kept by the abductor as a captive. In stereotypical kidnappings, the abductors ask for a ransom and at least act as though the teen will be returned to the family.

When a child under twelve years old goes missing, authorities don't question whether or not foul play is involved—it's pretty much a given. But with teens, law enforcement officers are less likely to immediately believe a child has been abducted. They take into consideration other scenarios, such as whether the teen has acted rebelliously or irresponsibly, before deciding whether a preteen or teen has run away or actually been abducted.

Many people think this is a Third World problem, but we are dealing with it in the United States as well.

- Most children who are abducted are between the ages of ten and fourteen, and more females than males are abducted.
- Females are targets of abductions 65 percent of the time.
- Abductors use a vehicle in 70 percent of abductions.
- More abductions occur between 2:00 p.m. and 7:00 p.m. than at any other time of the day—mainly because kids typically have less supervision after school.

Just because there's an abduction attempt doesn't mean all hope is lost. According to the National Center for Missing and Exploited Children,

- Teens who escape would-be abductors do something proactive as opposed to being compliant, passive, or polite.
- Of the teens who escaped an abduction, 53 percent walked or ran away from the suspect before any physical contact occurred.
- Another 26 percent of teens reported yelling, kicking, pulling away, or attracting attention.
- Twenty percent of the teens had help from a passerby or a parent who stopped the abduction.

So role-play this possibility with your teen. If your teenager is being forced to go with someone, he or she should scream that the person is not a friend and that they are being kidnapped. They need to yell loudly, struggle, and fight to get away. These are the actions of a prepared warrior heart!

You'd think that abductors who are successful at luring teens or children would be registered sex offenders, but only 13 percent of perpetrators were registered sex offenders at the time of the incident. However, in 21 percent of the abductions, there was a sexual assault or indecent exposure.[2]

Strategies

How do abductors lure kids? Some ask flattering opinion questions, like Maggie did with Celia. More often, though, the questions are about street directions or the locations of stores or restaurants. The four other popular lures utilized by abductors are

- offering a ride,
- offering candy or food,
- offering money, or
- asking for help finding an animal.

Heading to the mall with friends has been a kind of rite of passage in our culture, signaling that we believe our children are old enough to socialize without parental supervision. Whether kids are hanging out at the mall, the movie theater, or a restaurant, the risks are the same for your teenagers.

Your children can learn some basic safety rules to help them recognize safety issues when they are in public places.

Follow the rules. Many places post rules about when teenagers can visit, or may restrict visits of teenagers without parents. Malls have put these regulations in place to prevent children and teens from coming alone to the mall before a certain age. Come to an understanding with your kids about posted rules, and help them understand that if a place allows them to go only at certain times or with an adult, there is a good reason for it.

Set up a family secret word or phrase. Have a family meeting in which your family chooses a word or phrase that would not normally occur in conversation. Perhaps it is the fictitious name of a relative, such as "Aunt Susan." Or an unusual food such as rhubarb. If a stranger says to your teen that they have been sent to pick him or her up at school or a mall, or that they need to follow the stranger, the teen can ask for the secret word. If the person does not know it, the teen knows not to go with the stranger no matter what "emergency" he might have concocted. It can also be used as a code to let family members know if a kid is in trouble. For instance, if your child is uncomfortable at a friend's house, she can call you and ask if Aunt Susan is at their house.

Be aware of your surroundings. For teenagers in public places, generally strangers pose the greatest risk. Next time you are in a store or theater with your teen, show them how to be aware of who is around them and how to locate the closest place to seek adult help.

Teach a child of any age that if they are being followed or harassed in any way, they must leave the situation or seek help from a security officer. If your teenager is driving, teach them to look around before they get in or out of a car. If they look around and feel unsafe, they need to trust their gut. If your teen is walking out to a car and feels unsafe, he or she should go back into the mall or store and have a security guard walk him or her to the car. If, when they arrive at a location and the situation even "smells" unsafe, they should just drive away to a safe place such as a police station. Help your children identify where police stations are in your neighborhood.

Handle money and credit cards responsibly. Teenagers frequently don't recognize that they can make themselves targets by flashing cash or using a credit card to buy expensive purchases. Predators are watching for this. It's against the nature of a teenager, but they must be aware of their surroundings and try not to draw attention to themselves, their money, or their purchases.

Know your real friends. Talk with your kids about the difference between real friends and acquaintances. Real friends are people you have known for a long time, not people you have just met. Real friends are people who have earned your trust.

You know this but teenagers don't: Kids can't assess the honesty of people they have just met. They simply don't have the life experience to recognize when they are being deceived. Since teenagers don't have these skills, they need to avoid leaving public places with people they don't know well. Teach your teenagers to stay with real friends and not to leave public places like a mall even to walk to the parking lot with people who are not real friends.

Follow the "Rule of Threes." There's safety in numbers for your teen in public places such as malls. Enforce this rule: Your teen must stay with at least two other friends they know well. Real friends are the best protection against an abduction. Abductors who are trying to target teens for sex trafficking will look for teens they can separate from their friends. If they can't separate one person from a group, then predators will move on to another target.

Adults should ask adults for help. One of the most basic rules your teenagers should understand is that adults should ask only adults for help. Adults who ask teenagers for help or advice are not demonstrating healthy boundaries. If someone needs help, an adult is the one who will have the resources and life experience to know what to do. If an adult is asking a teenager for assistance, it should be a huge red flag for your child. Your child should redirect the adult to talk to another adult—and leave the situation immediately.

Trust your feelings. We process much more sensory information (sights, sounds, other stimuli) than we consciously know we are taking in. Because we can't consciously access all the sensory information, it doesn't mean our senses aren't communicating! We often have intuitive or gut feelings about situations. Always honor a child's gut feelings and congratulate them for leaving situations when they do not feel safe.

I've heard many stories of Christian friends who "had a feeling" that warned them. Seek out from your friends those who can tell your teen about dangerous situations that were averted because the Holy Spirit gave them an inexplicable warning.

Don't fall for compliments. Teens need to be aware that when someone is complimenting them or seeking their assistance, it should raise a red flag. Obviously there are some situations in which teens are complimented a lot, such as for winning an athletic event. However, they should be suspicious when someone is always complimenting them, or if the situation resembles the scenario of Celia and Maggie—a stranger seeking assistance.

Role-play with your child the difference between a compliment and flattery. A compliment is a gift. Flattery presents a bill to be paid. Even though it might not look like it at first, flattery is always someone trying to get someone else to give them something. It's a fake compliment, and it always comes with a big price tag in the end—because when you accept flattery, the other person believes you owe them something in return. It's designed to break down your defenses so you turn control of a situation over to the flatterer.

The Bible tells about a world-class flatterer named Absalom (2 Samuel 15:2–6). This prince wanted his father's kingdom, so he sat outside the gates, and when someone came to the city for justice in some matter, oily Absalom would soften them up by asking about their homeland. When they described their problem, he'd flatter them and tell them they had a good case. He'd shake hands with them, even kiss them, and promise he'd take care of it. He didn't want justice; he wanted power. And so, the Bible says, he "stole the hearts of the people of Israel," much to everyone's regret and disaster.

Hearts can indeed be stolen by flattery. Talk about it, and protect your child with a warrior heart that knows its own worth, and won't be moved by smooth words or deceptive appeals for help.

Messages for Your Teen

Keep nurturing that warrior heart. Kids can learn to safeguard themselves if you give them the tools. Keep them safe by giving them the information and support they need to make good decisions. Your teens should know about God's plan for sexuality in marriage and recognize sexual behaviors.

- Teens should know what sexual and emotional limits are healthy in a relationship and how to tell other people about those limits.

- Teenagers should recognize that it is dangerous if someone violates the emotional or sexual limits they have set, and speak up immediately.
- Let your teens know that they have the right at any point to say no to a sexual behavior.
- Teach your children safety skills for group gatherings. Teach them to pour their own beverage and keep it in their sight. Help them recognize that peers can put drugs or alcohol in their beverages.
- Teach your teenagers to be aware of where they are hanging out and to avoid places that keep them isolated from others. Teens may feel like they can take care of themselves, but they don't have the life experiences to recognize when they are in danger.
- Help your teens learn to trust their instincts. If they feel that a person or situation is not safe, they should leave immediately.
- Help your teens recognize that they need a back-up plan no matter where they go. This plan should include telling someone they trust where they are going. They should always have a person to call who will come immediately to get them.
- Teach your teens that technology can open the door to predators and allow them access to personal information.

Warning Signs of Abuse

The abused teen may
- have nightmares and/or images in their head about the assault;

- exhibit changes in eating patterns and experience weight gain or loss;
- have bruising or physical injuries;
- show changes in school performance or behavior;
- pay less attention to hygiene, appearance, or clothing style;
- show signs of depression, lack of energy, or changes in sleep;
- drink or use drugs; or
- engage in self-harm behaviors or have suicidal thoughts.

➡ WHAT YOU SHOULD DO

If you suspect your teen has been sexually or physically abused, remember not to overreact emotionally in front of your child. Let the child know you want to keep him or her safe—that it's your job, and you want to do it.

Take your concerns to a doctor, a social worker, or the police. You don't have to know that your child is not safe, you just have to suspect it to seek out professional assistance. And of course, don't leave your teen with any person they fear.

19

Abuse Using Technology

Unsupervised Access to Technology—Apps

When Jenna walks into my office with her daughter, Katie, the tension between them is like smoke in a room. Katie flings herself into a chair and crosses her arms. Jenna shoots Katie a look with reddened and puffy eyes, then sits down in the other chair. I look at them both.

"Would one of you like to tell me why you've come to see me today?"

Jenna looks at her daughter and says with exasperation, "Tell her why we are here. Go ahead."

"We are here because you *made* me come." Katie glares at her mother.

Obviously, if I am going to make progress in the session, I'll need to separate Jenna and Katie. The daughter is so angry that I decide to start by meeting with Jenna alone. I ask Katie to step into the waiting room for a while. She rolls her eyes, but goes.

"So you've brought Katie to see me," I begin once I sit down across from Jenna. "Can you give me some background?"

"Well, first of all, we have three kids, and she's been the hardest of all," Jenna begins. "She ignores every rule we have about devices—you know, phone, computer, electronics." She explains that she and her husband always monitored their teenagers' use of technology, from childhood days on. They routinely check the web browser, texts, and social media use of their children. At night they collect everyone's phones and devices and remove the power cord to the computers in the home. Then they keep the technology in their bedroom so the kids can't access it.

I nod. Smart parents.

"So," I probe, "how does she ignore your rules?"

"We thought she was okay with all of that. We started those rules with our older kids, and everyone just knew that's the way it was. But then we had a seminar at church about sexting. I didn't think I really needed that—we had our bases covered there." Jenna laughs a short, bitter laugh.

In the seminar, Jenna and her husband learned that teens were using apps that looked like calculators, calendars, and games, hiding the fact that users could text and send pictures and videos. Jenna took notes about the apps, but really didn't think that her children would be using them.

"But then a few days later, I'm lying in bed thinking about the seminar, and I decided to look through Katie's apps on her phone." She pantomimes a finger into her other palm. Stab, stab, stab.

"Everything looks okay until I get to the calculator." She throws her arms into the air in amazement, her eyes wide. "And then some stupid-sounding game." She stops for a moment. "So I find out Katie has been sending nude pictures to people I don't know. And then I check her tablet, same thing. Never heard of these people."

"What did you do?"

"I went in and woke her up. I showed her some of those pictures, on her own phone. I was furious!"

"How did Katie respond to that?"

"I was amazed. She didn't think it was a big deal. We argued for almost an hour about it—woke up everybody in the house. Bottom line, she didn't get to use the phone or tablet."

"But there's still a problem?"

"I didn't think so at first. She was mad, of course. I kept tabs on her computer use and thought things were getting better. But then I get a call from Julie's mom—that's Katie's best friend—and it turns out that Katie has been borrowing her friend's phone. Katie put some of those same apps on Julie's phone. Sex texts. Julie found them, then Julie's mom got involved. She got as mad as I did, and told Julie that Katie could never use her phone again. Even if it made Katie mad, and I think you've seen her mad now."

"What do you have in mind for me to do with Katie when I meet with her?"

"Talk some sense into her! Tell her how dangerous it is to use apps like that! Quit sexting! Get her to stop sending nude pictures!"

"I have to tell you this can't happen right away," I tell her. "It will take some time for Katie to trust me to address some of those issues."

Indeed, when Jenna leaves and Katie comes into my office, she seems more angry and more distant than before, as if she is talking from somewhere else in a language of clipped rage.

"What did my mom tell you?"

"I'd rather hear from you what you think I need to know."

Katie begins, and I am surprised that the events she described are pretty much the same as recounted by her mom. The big difference is that Katie thinks her mom is overreacting.

"Everybody does it," Katie says. "Sexting isn't a big deal. The pictures, they're not a big deal. Mom can't get that through her head."

I consider to myself the fact that Katie attends church regularly, and is active in her youth group. I try to reconcile this knowledge with this indignant, offended young woman and the pictures and texts she sends. But as she continues to talk about her relationship with her mom, the importance in her life of her phone and other devices, she seems to calm a bit. As we near the end of our session, I have some hope.

"Would you like to come back and talk again?"

She thinks for a minute. "Only if you can fix my mom. She is a hot mess."

We bargain back and forth a bit about the details, give and take, give and take. In the end, we schedule more meetings. Gradually, through several counseling sessions I am able to help Katie recognize how dangerous sexting is and that she can find other ways to connect with her peers. We also meet repeatedly with her mother, and eventually communication and trust improves between them.

Those Devices

A Pew Research study in 2018 found that 95 percent of teens have access to a smartphone, and 45 percent say they are online almost constantly. Roughly half of teens use Facebook, but many more use YouTube, Instagram, or Snapchat. Ninety percent of teens say they play video games on a computer, game console, or cell phone. Game consoles also provide access to the Internet and to social media.

While kids are using technology daily, parents often don't monitor what their teens do online. A 2016 Pew Research Center survey found that only about half of parents said they had ever checked their children's phone calls and text messages or even friended their kids on social media. They were even less likely to use tech-based tools to monitor their teens or block certain apps.

The key to keeping your teens safe online is to talk with them and explain to them the dangers of interacting with people they do not know online, or of people getting information about them online. Emphasize that the rules you put in place about technology are there to protect them, not punish them. Hopefully, you started the discussions about technology when they were younger, so they expect you to monitor their use of technology to help keep them safe.

Tools for Parents

1. Develop a written contract with your teens about Internet use both at home and outside the home. Specify acceptable use and unacceptable use and the consequences for violating the contract.

2. Continue to set age-appropriate filters for teenagers. Parents seem more aware of using filters for children, but teens need filters as well. Change passwords often.

3. Investigate monitoring software. Such software is affordable and helps us monitor everything our children are accessing online. We wouldn't send our children out into the real world without supervision. Similarly, we should not send them out into the virtual world without supervision.

4. Set time limits for the use of technology. Too much technology use is not good for teens or adults. Limit the use of technology at mealtime and at night. Expect your children to engage with you in your home.

5. Don't allow your children to use chat rooms or video chat with strangers. Similarly, your children should not text or message any person they do not know in the real world.

6. Utilize parental controls on your child's mobile phone and other devices. Parental controls should be utilized on all Internet-enabled devices, including desktops, laptops, tablets, gaming consoles, Alexa, and music devices.

What Parents Can Do

1. Supervise the photos and videos your kids post and send online. Make sure the metadata that provides location is stripped from the photos. Watermark photos of your family and teach your children to watermark photos they post. If someone wants to steal or alter photos from you, it will be harder if you have a personal watermark covering the photo.

2. Have full access to your teenager's phones and devices. Teenagers without a lot of life experience don't have the judgment to know whether they should trust someone or some organization online. Routinely go through your child's smartphone and open up all the apps to see what your teens are doing.

3. Know all of your teen's social media account names and passwords. Network with the parents of your teen's friends so that all of you are monitoring social media. Frequently teens will add social media accounts under other names and still be interacting with questionable people. When all the parents monitor social media, you can generally catch teens who are adding extra accounts.

4. Teach your teens the importance of not sharing passwords with their friends or other people. While you need

to know their passwords, no one else should know them. Teens need to be careful that they do not write down usernames and passwords in notebooks that can be lost or stolen, or enter or write them in public places where other people could see them.

5. Only add online friends that are real-life friends. While it can be very tempting to meet new people online, it is also very dangerous. It's too easy for online predators to fool teens. Teens don't have the skills to figure out that online friends may not actually be who they say they are.

6. Teach your teens to be aware of what they post online and who can see it. Find out how to check privacy settings on apps and social media and teach your teens how to check privacy settings. Teens may believe they are sharing information only with friends when they are really sharing it with strangers. Help your teens recognize the importance of not posting where they are and where they live for safety reasons. Teach them how to protect personal information posted online and to follow the same rules with respect to the personal information of others.

Communicating with a Sexual Predator Online

With the mass expansion of the Internet and social media, children are more and more accessible to online predators, and it is imperative that parents and guardians protect their children from these channels of exploitation.

Tweens and teenagers are bull's-eye targets of sexual predators who hide behind computer screens. There, they feel invincible and think they are less likely to be caught. But by teaching your child that the computer and social media sites they use are not private—

nothing on the Internet is ever truly private—and that you and others can see what they are sending, you take the essential first step to preventing your child's exploitation by online predators.

Online, kids use social media websites or chat rooms to talk to friends, make new ones, or just pass time, and sometimes they purposely look for sexually explicit information. Pornography is sometimes used as a gateway for sexual predators to show their victims that sex between children and adults is "normal." Through being desensitized to porn, teens are inclined to open up and get closer to the predator because they don't feel like they are doing anything wrong. Some predators send their victims letters, photographs and, in extreme cases, even plane tickets for the child to travel and meet them.

One of the first and most apparent warning signs that your child may be communicating with an online predator is if they spend unusually long periods of time on the Internet. Be alert if your child begins to withdraw from the family, as this may be a warning sign that a predator is interacting with your child: Online predators try to manipulate a teen away from communicating with family so they can influence him or her.

Another dangerous warning sign that your child is communicating with an online predator is if you begin to find pornography of any kind on your child's computer or if they begin to receive calls or gifts from unknown callers or senders. Predators send gifts to potential victims in hopes of meeting face-to-face.

Even Jesus had a false friend. Though He was an adult and knew the hearts of people, His close friend Judas hung around because Judas wanted something. In this case, this false friend wanted access to the money that had been contributed to Jesus' ministry.

But Judas betrayed his friend Jesus for even more money. If you'd been watching Judas in the Garden of Gethsemane when he came with a small army where Jesus was praying, you'd have seen a predator in action. Instead of being upfront about his motives, Judas pointed Him out to the arresting army with a kiss on Jesus' cheek. Instead of protecting Jesus, this false friend sold Him out.

But Jesus had a warrior heart too. He knew how unreliable Judas was, how self-serving. Unlike teens (and us adults as well!), He could see into that traitorous heart. Even in surrendering to betrayal, Jesus did what He did to protect others. He knew the long game.

And because He knows what it's like to be betrayed, He can strengthen your warrior heart too.

That's your role as a parent. You know the long game and can protect your children against those who would literally or figuratively kiss them to betray their innocence.

Messages for Your Teen

Keep nurturing that warrior heart. Kids can learn to safeguard themselves if you give them the tools. Keep them safe by giving them the information and support they need to make good decisions. Your teens should know about God's plan for sexuality in marriage and recognize sexual behaviors.

- Teens should know what sexual and emotional limits are healthy in a relationship and how to tell other people about those limits.
- Teenagers should recognize that it is dangerous if someone violates the emotional or sexual limits they have set, and speak up immediately.
- Let your teens know that they have the right at any point to say no to a sexual behavior.

- Teach your children safety skills for group gatherings. Teach them to pour their own beverage and keep it in their sight. Help them recognize that peers can put drugs or alcohol in their beverages.

- Teach your teenagers to be aware of where they are hanging out and to avoid hanging out in places that keep them isolated from others. Teens may feel like they can take care of themselves, but they don't have the life experiences to recognize when they are in danger.

- Help your teens learn to trust their instincts. If they feel that a person or situation is not safe, they should leave immediately.

- Help your teens recognize that they need a back-up plan no matter where they go. This plan should include telling someone they trust where they are going. They should always have a person to call who will come immediately to get them.

- Teach your teens that technology can open the door to predators and allow them access to personal information.

Warning Signs of Abuse

The abused teen may
- have nightmares and/or images in their head about the assault;
- exhibit changes in eating patterns and experience weight gain or loss;
- have bruising or physical injuries;
- show changes in school performance or behavior;

- pay less attention to hygiene, appearance, or clothing style;
- show signs of depression, lack of energy, or changes in sleep;
- drink or use drugs; or
- engage in self-harm behaviors or have suicidal thoughts.

➡ WHAT YOU SHOULD DO

If you suspect your teen has been sexually or physically abused, remember not to overreact emotionally in front of your child. Let the child know you want to keep him or her safe—that it's your job, and you want to do it.

Take your concerns to a doctor, a social worker, or the police. You don't have to know that your child is not safe, you just have to suspect it to seek out professional assistance. And of course, don't leave your teen with any person they fear.

Conclusion

There's a remarkable—and chilling—story in the Bible about how evil starts, with those who "plan iniquity . . . those who plot evil on their beds! At morning's light they carry it out *because it is in their power to do it*" (Micah 2:1, emphasis added).

Now that you've read about the way sexual predators work, you know it involves deception and misdirection and careful scheming in the dark moments of their minds. It doesn't just happen. They are not just overtaken in the moment with a new thought of hurting your child. Sexual abuse is the end of a premeditated process, an idea that takes on flesh.

But the same process works for you. I hope I've gotten your warrior heart fired up so now that you know about predators, you are the one who will strategize—to protect. If what you've read keeps you up at night, use that time to pray, to set up safeguards, to practice how to start protective conversations with your child, to preclude bad situations before they even happen.

Remember, though, before you set these procedures and safeguards in place, your heart has to arm itself with resolution, to be extra vigilant, to be repeatedly inconvenienced, to go the extra mile.

Then you can arm your child with a warrior heart.

Everyone knows how toxic mold works. Spores come into a receptive place, one that has what it needs to feed and grow. As long as it is dark, undisturbed, and has access to what it needs to grow in that lightless environment, it will keep growing.

Not until someone removes access to what mold seeks and exposes it to light will it stop spreading. Usually, remediation works on whatever has been affected by it, but it's always costly and difficult. Sometimes the structure is demolished.

Similarly, families, churches, and other organizations are damaged when something dark and hidden is allowed to grow. They too can fall apart, due to the actions of one predator with an agenda.

As with mold, prevention is the smart course of action. Sexual predators follow a pattern so identifiable that it's almost a cliché. It's true, a very small percentage of them just seem to spring into existence in the shopping mall or online. But almost all are slow-working and methodical. They look good. They are helpful. They are likeable. They are patient. They have something you want. They are the ones who will help relieve you of some of the burdens of your busy schedule or your responsibilities of parenthood.

Remember, statistically speaking, they probably have offended before and gotten away with it. This isn't their first rodeo. Even if you've checked references and they're clear, that does not constitute an endorsement—the overwhelming majority of sexual predators never face legal charges. They have operated in the past because people didn't watch, didn't question, didn't follow up and speak up about those first feelings of something "just not quite right."

You must, and *you* will.

If you refuse to surrender your parental rights to a group or an individual, if you're involved and watching, and if what you see looks like grooming, it probably is. The innocent and bumbling adult in such a scenario might not like being watched or questioned, but they have nothing to hide. If they care about kids, they will agree that extra vigilance is a good thing. They will want to protect, and live within, boundaries.

The predator will not like being under a microscope, may become aggressive in self-defense, and if confronted, probably will move on to more receptive targets. Again, so common a pattern as to be a cliché.

You might ask, "Aren't you setting up barriers between well-meaning Christians?" Between good people who have pure minds and motives—how can you tell the difference? How do you manage risk?

In adult-to-adult relationships, you yourself can take risks with the helpful, kind person. You can be as open and accepting of them in a relationship as your conscience requires.

You take the consequences. But don't let your child take any such risk.

But what about the Christian necessity of forgiveness? Jesus himself said that if we don't forgive, we can't expect forgiveness.

What do we do with the offender?

In our society, there are penalties for grievous offenses. Convicted criminals do not give up their citizenship, for instance, but they forfeit the right to vote. Similarly, we may choose to forgive, but the predator must always forfeit access to our children.

Sins against children exact a terrible price on those they enthrall. Like alcoholics who are put back into full-blown drunkenness by one single drink, predators have been irreparably changed. The alcoholic can't go back to a "normal" relationship with liquor. Reformed pedophiles may want to do better, but some switch flipped and they can't go back to unsupervised relationships with your kids.

Ever. Under any circumstances.

Are there exceptions to this rule? In all my years of practice, I don't know of a single one. With such odds, are you willing to risk the safety and emotional stability and perhaps even the souls of your children to give someone that second chance?

And here's another caveat, tried and true: The repentant, reformed pedophile won't seek access to your child. He knows it is far too dangerous for him, and for your child.

I wrote this book using my case files and concentrating on scenarios of where and how abuse happens. Of course, we all have some built-in alert system regarding the Internet, or about sending our kids to a shopping mall, but most of us still choose to have the Internet and malls as part of our lives. We don't eliminate them from our lives, but we must manage them.

We usually have no such alert system about family or close friends. We think we know them. We have no such alert system about church and parachurch organizations like church camp either. These are what we think of as low risk, at least as compared with a mall or surfing the Internet. But the situations that pose the greatest risk are those where people close to you are predators—statistically abuse is *more* likely to happen in a church than in a mall.

Why? You come to a church as a hospital to recover from the world, not to scope out predators. You want to trust and be trusted. Your guard is down. You want peace, love, and kumbaya. And predators know that.

Still, we can take great comfort in the fact that, with godly counseling and support, children can recover from sexual abuse. We can rejoice because so many people stand ready to help and support you and your family no matter what happens.

Ephesians chapter 6 reminds us that this isn't a flesh-and-blood tussle, it's a supernatural, epic, cosmic battle.

Put on the full armor of God, so that you can take your stand against the devil's schemes. For our struggle is not against flesh and blood, but against the rulers, against the authorities, against the powers of this dark world and against the spiritual forces of evil in the heavenly realms. Therefore put on the full armor of God, so that when the day of evil comes, you may be able to stand your ground, and after you have done everything, to stand. Stand firm then, with the belt of truth buckled around your waist, with the breastplate of righteousness in place, and with your feet fitted with the readiness that comes from the gospel of peace. In addition to all this, take up the shield of faith, with which you can extinguish all the flaming arrows of the evil one. Take the helmet of salvation and the sword of the Spirit, which is the word of God.

And pray in the Spirit on all occasions with all kinds of prayers and requests. With this in mind, *be alert* and always keep on praying for all the Lord's people.

Ephesians 6:11–18, italics added

We aren't alone! We have supernatural help!

For though we live in the world, we do not wage war as the world does. The weapons we fight with are not the weapons of the world. On the contrary, they have divine power to demolish strongholds. We demolish arguments and every pretension that sets itself up against the knowledge of God, and we take captive every thought to make it obedient to Christ.

2 Corinthians 10:3–5

That's why your child needs a warrior heart, because we've got a war to fight. When the Ephesians passage tells you to put on armor, God's not kidding.

You're in for the fight of your life, and this isn't just about some cute Sunday school drawing of a soldier. Choose your weapons and pay the price for the finest ones. Sharpen them. Check the armor and helmet for fit.

You are that warrior. Your child is that warrior.

Charge!

Recommended Resources

DVD or online streaming video

Reducing the Risk: A Child Sexual Abuse Awareness Program at http://store.churchlawtodaystore.com/reducing
risk1.html.

Website

The National Child Traumatic Stress Network at https://
www.nctsn.org/

Apps

Kaspersky Safe Kids
TrueMotion Family Safe Driving
Life360 Family Locator
Safety for Kids
SPIN Safe Browser

Previous Publications by Dr. Robinson Related to This Book

Therapeutic Children's Coloring Books

The Safe Family Coloring Book, 2nd ed. (Dawson Parker Publishing, 2013)

The Safe Touch Coloring Book, 2nd ed. (Dawson Parker Publishing, 2013)

God Made Me: The Safe Touch Coloring Book, 2nd ed. (Dawson Parker Publishing, 2013)

El libro de colorear sobre tactos seguros (Dawson Parker Publishing, 2012)

Previous Publications by Dr. Scott Related to This Book

The Hinge of Your History: The Phases of Faith (Create-Space, 2010)

The Mona Lisa Mirror Mystery (Cruciform Press, 2018)

Notes

Introduction: Creating a Warrior Heart

1. David Eggert and Mike Householder, "Larry Nassar Sentenced to 40 to 175 Years in Prison; Judge Says 'I Just Signed Your Death Warrant,'" *Chicago Tribune*, January 24, 2018, https://www.chicagotribune.com/sports/international/ct-larry-nassar-gymnastics-sentencing-20180124-story.html.

2. Jennifer L. Truman, PhD, "National Crime Victimization Survey," *Criminal Victimization, 2010*, U.S. Department of Justice, Office of Justice Programs, Bureau of Justice Statistics, September 2011, http://bjs.ojp.usdoj.gov/content/pub/pdf/cv10.pdf.

3. U.S. Department of Health and Human Services, Administration for Children and Families, *Child Maltreatment*, 2013, https://www.acf.hhs.gov/sites/default/files/cb/cm2012.pdf.

4. American Psychological Association, "Understanding Child Sexual Abuse," December 2011, https://www.apa.org/pi/about/newsletter/2011/12/sexual-abuse.

5. American Psychological Association, "Understanding Child Sexual Abuse."

6. Canadian Centre for Child Protection, *Child Sexual Abuse: It Is Your Business*, November 1, 2012, 10, https://www.cybertip.ca/pdfs/C3P_ChildSexualAbuse_ItIsYourBusiness_en.pdf.

7. Canadian Centre for Child Protection, *Child Sexual Abuse: It Is Your Business*, 10.

8. Debra Allnock, "Children and Young People Disclosing Sexual Abuse," Child Protection Research Department, NSPCC Fresh Start, April 2010, http://www.childmatters.org.nz/file/Diploma-Readings/Block-2/Sexual-Abuse/3.4-children-and-young-people-disclosing-sexual-abuse-updated.pdf.

9. American Psychological Association, "Understanding Child Sexual Abuse."

Chapter 4: Abuse by Authority Figure: The Sitter

1. Born between 1995 and 2012, iGens have poorer emotional health, thanks to new media. Jean Twenge in *iGen: Why Today's Super-Connected Kids Are Growing Up Less Rebellious, More Tolerant, Less Happy—and Completely Unprepared for Adulthood—and What That Means for the Rest of Us*, finds that new media are making teens lonelier, more anxious, and more depressed, and it's undermining their social skills and even their sleep. She also notes that "iGen'ers are growing up more slowly: 18-year-olds now act like 15-year-olds used to, and 13-year-olds like 10-year-olds" (p. 3).

These iGens "grew up with cell phones, had an Instagram page before they started high school, and do not remember a time before the Internet," writes Twenge (p. 2). They spend five to six hours a day texting, chatting, gaming, web surfing, streaming and sharing videos, and hanging out online. While other observers have equivocated about the impact, Twenge is clear: More than two hours a day of such activity raises the risk for serious mental health problems.

Dr. Steven Bonner and Dr. Dean Culpepper assessed the moral development of college freshmen with the DIT-2, and a preliminary analysis shows that scores are at or below scores of high school freshmen sixteen years ago.

Source: Steven Bonner and Dean Culpepper, "Extended Midadolescence & Entering College Students: Quantitative Evidence of Diminished Logical and Moral Cognitive Development," Association of Youth Ministry Educators, National Meeting, Chicago, IL, 2013.

Chapter 5: Abuse by Peer: The Small Group Bible Study

1. David Finkelhor and Anne Shattuck, "Characteristics of Crimes against Juveniles," May 2012, Crimes Against Children Research Center, University of New Hampshire, http://www.unh.edu/ccrc/pdf/CV26_Revised%20Characteristics%20of%20Crimes%20against%20Juveniles_5-2-12.pdf.

Chapter 6: Abuse by Family Member or Trusted Friend: The Cousin

1. Judith Herman, "Father–daughter incest," *Professional Psychology* 12, no. 1 (1981): 76–80, http://dx.doi.org/10.1037/0735-7028.12.1.76.

2. Chart adapted and updated from S. K. Wurtele and C. L. Miller-Perrin, *Preventing Sexual Abuse* (Lincoln, NE: University of Nebraska Press, 1992), 1–54.

Chapter 13: Abuse Involving Technology: The Wikipedia Ambush

1. There are many online resources available that describe how to strip the metadata from photos; one can be found at https://us.norton.com/internetsecurity-how-to-how-to-remove-gps-and-other-metadata-locations-from-photos.html.

Chapter 14: Ages Twelve and Older: What Your Adolescent Should Know

1. Joan R. Kahn and Kathryn A. London, "Premarital Sex and the Risk of Divorce," *Journal of Marriage and the Family*, 53 (1991): 845-855.

2. Kirk Johnson, Lauren Noyes, and Robert Rector, "Sexually Active Teenagers Are More Likely to Be Depressed and to Attempt Suicide," *The Heritage Foundation*, June 3, 2005, https://www.heritage.org/education/report/sexually-active-teenagers-are-more-likely-be-depressed-and-attempt-suicide.

Chapter 16: Abuse by Family/Trusted Friend: The Coach

1. Danielle Paquette and Weiyi Cai, "Why American Teenagers Are Having Much Less Sex," *The Washington Post*, July 22, 2015, https://www.washingtonpost.com/news/wonk/wp/2015/07/22/why-american-teenagers-are-having-much-less-sex/?utm_term=.5d0fc0bf37de. Actual data and quotation from the CDC at Joyce C. Abma, PhD, and Gladys M. Martinez, PhD, "Sexual Activity and Contraceptive Use Among Teenagers in the United States, 2011–2015," *National Health Statistics Reports* No.104, June 22, 2017, https://www.cdc.gov/nchs/data/nhsr/nhsr104.pdf.

2. The National Online Resource Center on Violence Against Women, Pornography and Sexual Violence, https://vawnet.org/sites/default/files/materials/files/2016-09/AR_PornAndSV.pdf.

Chapter 17: Abuse by Peer: Dating Violence

1. J. A. Grunbaum, L. Kann, S. Kinchen, et al., "Youth Risk Behavior Surveillance—United States, 2003," *Morbidity and Mortality Weekly Report*, May 21, 2004, 53(SS02); 1-96, http://www.cdc.gov/mmwr/preview/mmwrhtml/ss5302a1.htm.

2. Centers for Disease Control and Prevention, National Center for Injury Prevention and Control, Division of Violence Prevention, "Dating Matters: Strategies to Promote Healthy Teen Relationships," http://www.cdc.gov/violenceprevention/pdf/datingmatters_flyer_2012-a.pdf.

3. S. Hayes and S. Jeffries, "Why Do They Keep Going Back? Exploring Women's Discursive Experiences of Intimate Partner Abuse," *International Journal of Criminology and Sociology*, 2013, 2, 57–71; C. Power, T. Koch, D. Kralik, and D. Jackson, "Lovestruck: Women, Romantic Love and Intimate Partner Violence," *Contemporary Nursing* 21, no. 2 (May 2006):174–85; S. Puente and D. Cohen, "Jealousy and the Meaning (or Nonmeaning) of Violence," *Personality and Social Psychology Bulletin* 29, no. 4 (2006): 449–460; Adewale Rotimi, "Violence in the Family: A Preliminary Investigation and Overview of Wife Battering in Africa," *Journal of International Women's Studies*, 9, no. 1 (2007): 234–252.

4. Centers for Disease Control and Prevention, "Teen Dating Violence," https://www.edc.gov/features/datingviolence/.

5. National Judicial Education Program, *The Dynamics and Consequences of Teen Dating Violence*, https://www.legalmomentum.org/sites/default/files/reports/NJEP%20TDV%20Information%20and%20Resources%20Sheets%20Collected%20Document.pdf.

6. National Judicial Education Program, *The Dynamics and Consequences of Teen Dating Violence*.

7. National Judicial Education Program, *The Dynamics and Consequences of Teen Dating Violence.*

8. National Judicial Education Program, *The Dynamics and Consequences of Teen Dating Violence.*

Chapter 18: Abuse by Strangers: Malls and Other Public Places

1. National Incidence Studies of Missing, Abducted, Runaway, and Thrownaway Children.

2. Lawrence A. Greenfield, "Sex Offenses and Offenders: An Analysis of Data on Rape and Sexual Assault," Bureau of Justice Statistics Executive Summary, January 1997, U.S. Department of Justice.

Beth Robinson, EdD, is a professor of psychology at Lubbock Christian University and a visiting lecturer in the Clinical Mental Health Counseling program at Harding University; she was previously a professor of pediatrics at Texas Tech University Health Sciences Center. She is a licensed professional counselor, an approved supervisor for licensed professional counselors, and a certified school counselor. She has used those credentials to work with abused and traumatized children for more than twenty-five years as a counselor. Beth has also lived with foster and adoptive children in her home and has written books for professionals, parents, and children.

Latayne C. Scott, PhD, is the author of over two dozen books, fiction and nonfiction, and hundreds of published shorter works. She is the recipient of Pepperdine University's Distinguished Christian Service Award for her writing. She is married and lives in Albuquerque.